11th GRADE READY

EXPERT ADVICE TO HELP PARENTS NAVIGATE THE YEAR AHEAD

EDITED BY
TIMOTHY M. DOVE

A READY GUIDE

PARENT **READY.**

PARENT READY.

2024 Edition
Copyright © 2024 Parent Ready, Inc.

Parent Ready supports the right to free expression and the value of copyright. The purpose of copyright is to encourage the creation of works that enrich our culture.

All rights reserved. No part of this book may be reprinted or reproduced in any form or by any electronic, mechanical, or other means, now known or hereafter invented, including photocopying, recording, and information storage and retrieval, without the prior written permission of the publisher, except in the case of brief quotations embodied in critical articles and reviews.

Published by Parent Ready, Inc.
8 East Windsor Avenue
Alexandria, Virginia 22301
https://parentready.com

Parent Ready and design are trademarks of Parent Ready, Inc.

The publisher is not responsible for websites (or their contents) that are not owned by the publisher.

ISBN: 979-8-9893392-1-1 (paperback)
ISBN: 979-8-9893392-5-9 (e-book)

Bulk purchases: Quantity discounts are available. Please make inquiries via https://gradeready.guide.

Table of Contents

Contributors vii
Foreword xiii
   Dr. Alysha Collins

Introduction. xvii
   Timothy M. Dove

Chapter 1: How Is 11th Grade Different from 10th Grade? 1
   Ways to support your student during this transitional year
   David Bosso

Chapter 2: How Is an 11th Grader Different from a 10th Grader? . . 9
   What to expect from your 200-month-old
   Andrea Sachs

Chapter 3: How Does Inclusion and Belonging Help
   My Student? 17
   How to encourage both in academic and social settings
   Efren Villalobos

Chapter 4: Different Learning Styles and Accommodations 27
   How understanding the way your student learns can help them
   John Skretta

Chapter 5: Leaning into Homework and Study Skills 37
   How can I help my student succeed in the classroom?
   Marcy Dovholuk

Chapter 6: Motivating High School Students and
   Overcoming Procrastination 45
   How to help your teen avoid procrastination
   Jillian Huber

Chapter 7: Reality Bites 53
    How to overcome academic hurdles and prep for
        high-stakes exams
    Heidi Edwards

Chapter 8: Why Can't My Teen Get Along with Their Teachers? . . . 61
    Scripts and strategies to support your student
    Al Rabanera

Chapter 9: Building Positive Student-Teacher Relationships. 69
    How to navigate conflict and solicit good letters of
        recommendation
    John Skretta

Chapter 10: Online Presence 77
    How to help your junior start building a career-ready profile
    Timothy M. Dove

Chapter 11: Finding Passions…In and Out of School 87
    How to help identify and support your teen's interests
    Stacey McAdoo

Chapter 12: Developing Passions in Sports. 95
    How to support your student-athlete
    Mandy Manning

Chapter 13: Is Your Student a Budding Artist? 103
    How to help your teen pursue a life in the arts
    Lisa Hirkaler

Chapter 14: Ready for 12th Grade? 111
    How to support your soon-to-be high school senior
    Lori Knisley

This series of books is dedicated to all those who contribute to the education and support of young people. I was lucky enough to be a classroom teacher for 32 years. I owe a lot of my effectiveness to those who worked with me and those who taught me so much over the years, especially two master educators, Jenelle and Mark Dove, my parents. We all have teachers who made important contributions to our formal and informal education. Our parents and classroom teachers are on the front lines to encourage, question, teach, and celebrate our students. I want to thank all my colleagues who agreed to be a part of this project. We can always learn from one another, and having many voices in this conversation is so helpful. Thank you to all the educators who are still engaged in this sacred trust.

—Timothy M. Dove

Contributors

Editor

Timothy M. Dove, 2011 and 2012 Ohio State Teacher of the Year, was a 7th- and 8th-grade teacher for 32 years. He also was an adjunct professor at The Ohio State University for 20 years, working with MEd students in secondary social studies. During the last seven years of his K–12 career, he was part of a leadership team that designed a new public middle school with an emphasis on student voice, student choice, mastery, and a connection to community and service. Since retiring in 2013, he has been a consultant with Battelle for Kids in Hong Kong, Learning Forward, the Council of Chief State School Officers (CCSSO), and the Collaboration for Effective Educator Development, Accountability, and Reform (CEEDAR) Center, working with educators to better serve each and every student.

Contributors

David Bosso is the 2012 Connecticut Teacher of the Year and National Secondary Social Studies Teacher of the Year and a 2019 inductee into the National Teachers Hall of Fame. Over the course of his career, he has traveled to Africa, Asia, the Middle East, and Europe to work with international peers and to enrich students' understanding of global issues. He serves as the president of the Connecticut Teacher of the Year Council and is a past president of the Connecticut Council for the Social Studies. Bosso holds master's degrees from the University of Hartford and Central Connecticut State University and a doctorate from American International College.

Dr. Alysha Collins is an internationally certified school psychologist and certified administrator who enjoys supporting students, teachers, and their families. Collins obtained her doctorate in educational leadership and an educational specialist degree in school psychology. Her dissertation included studying hope during COVID-19. She is an adjunct instructor of university psychology classes and consults with organizations on mental health, educational research, and well-being in the workplace. Collins likes to apply her experience in trauma, hope, positive psychology, mindfulness, and diversity, equity, and inclusion to all her work. She is based in London, England.

Marcy Dovholuk is a high school assistant principal in Exeter, New Hampshire. She has been working in public schools for more than 30 years. She enjoys building relationships with students and parents, and enjoys her work immensely. Previously she was a reading specialist and a curriculum coordinator. She loves teaching and learning with children of all ages. Dovholuk recently completed her doctorate in educational leadership. She holds a certificate of advanced graduate studies (C.A.G.S.) in educational leadership, as well as a master's degree in education. She has completed coursework at the University of New Hampshire and programs at Harvard Graduate School of Education. When Dovholuk isn't working at school, she can be found at the beach, enjoying walks, reading, writing, or painting on canvas.

National Board-Certified **Heidi Edwards** has taught for 23 years. She teaches physical science, Advanced Placement biology, botany, and biotechnology at Oakwood High School in Oakwood, Ohio. She is active in her school culture as science department chair, teacher mentor, student council advisor, and cheer coordinator. Her passion for STEM led to opportunities to fly high-altitude missions aboard NASA's SOFIA observatory and selection as a 2023–24 CDC Science Ambassador fellow. Edwards served Air Camp USA as the curriculum specialist, leading to recognition as the 2012 National Air Force Association Teacher of the Year runner-up and the 2018 National Aviation Hall of Fame A. Scott Crossfield Aerospace Education Award winner.

Lisa Hirkaler has an MA from Columbia University Teachers College and is a National Board-Certified art teacher for adolescents and young adults. She received the 2016 New Jersey County Teacher of the Year award and is a reader/rater/grader for the Advanced Placement Art History exam. As an affiliate with the National Consortium on Teaching about Asia (NCTA), she travels, presents, and writes about her passion for Asian art and architecture. Hirkaler is also a professional artist, affiliated with Pleiades Gallery in New York City.

Jillian Huber is in her 19th year in education at Annawan High School in Annawan, Illinois, where she teaches English language arts. She is also a reading adjunct professor at Black Hawk College. Huber has worked for the National Education Association over the last 10 years as a Great Public Schools facilitator, edCommunities facilitator and coordinator, and a blended learning coordinator and facilitator. She enjoys reading and learning and working with other educators all around the nation. She also runs the Fellowship of Christian Athletes at her school and coaches junior high volleyball. She and her husband, Matt, keep very busy with their four boys.

Lori (Michalec) Knisley, the 2015 Ohio Teacher of the Year, works for Tallmadge City Schools, a suburban district of 2,500 students in Northeast Ohio. Knisley began a hybrid administrative-teaching position in the 2023–24 school year. After 22 years of teaching high school English, Knisley now serves as the Tallmadge High School testing coordinator and teaches two courses she developed under her

K–12 gifted/talented license to incorporate social-emotional learning and project-based/problem-based learning for 6th- and 7th-grade students at Tallmadge Middle School. Her goal is to empower students and prepare them for high school success.

Mandy Manning, the 2018 Washington State and National Teacher of the Year, advocates for educators, public schools, and students as the digital content specialist for the Washington Education Association. She served 21 years in the classroom as the first teacher for newly arrived refugee and immigrant students at Ferris High School in the Newcomer Center in Spokane, Washington. She serves on several education-related boards, including the Spectrum Center Board, serving the LGBTQ+ community in Spokane. Manning is co-author of *Creating a Sense of Belonging for Immigrant and Refugee Students: Strategies for K–12 Educators*. Her book, *50 Strategies for Teaching Multilingual Learners*, will be published by Teacher Created Materials in spring 2024.

Stacey McAdoo, 2019 Arkansas Teacher of the Year, is the executive director for Teach Plus Arkansas. Previously, she spent 19 years in the Little Rock School District as an accomplished classroom practitioner, college and career readiness coordinator, and lead secondary novice mentor teacher for the entire district. As a professional development facilitator for more than two decades, she designs and leads sessions that focus on best practices, instructional strategies, empowerment of student and teacher voice, promotion of equity, and the success of diverse learners. McAdoo is the founder of The Writeous Poets (a spoken word and youth advocacy collective), a board member of the Central Arkansas Library System, and a member of the National Arts in Education Advisory Council. McAdoo holds a BA in professional and technical writing, an MA in teaching, and an EdS in curriculum, instruction, and assessments. She lives in Little Rock with her husband, Leron, and they are the proud parents of Norel and Jamee. Visit her blog at stillstacey.com to learn more about her.

Al Rabanera, EdD, is a high school math teacher at La Vista High School in Fullerton, California. Rabanera is an advocate for educators and helped develop and implement new programs that promote teacher retention and encourage new generations of students to pursue careers in teaching. He has served on the board of directors for North Orange County United Teachers and the California Teachers Association Institute for Teaching and is on the board for the Council for the Accreditation of Educator Preparation. Rabanera was one of five educators to receive the Horace Mann Award for Teaching Excellence in 2017 and was an NEA Foundation Global Learning Fellow. In 2018, he received the Distinguished Alumni of the Year for the College of Education at California State University, Fullerton. In 2019–20, he served as a Teach Plus California Policy Fellow and is currently a Senior National Policy Advisory Board member. Rabanera earned his doctorate from the University of Southern California. He is married to Cassandra and they have a son, Nehemiah, and a daughter, Aurora.

Andrea Sachs has been a faculty member at St. Paul Academy and Summit School since 2000. She has taught history courses throughout her tenure, and from 2013–2019 she also worked as a college counselor. In addition to the 11th-grade introductory U.S. history course, she has taught senior electives in historiography, women's history, the history of social movements, and the history of medicine. She has served on the executive board of the Organization of American Historians and the Teacher Advisory Council of the National Constitution Center.

Dr. John Skretta, 2017 Nebraska Superintendent of the Year, is the chief administrator for Educational Service Unit 6, headquartered in Milford, Nebraska, which delivers professional development, student services, and technology infrastructure and support to 16 public school districts across five counties. Prior to serving in his current role, Dr. Skretta was a superintendent, assistant superintendent, and high school principal. He began his education career as a high school English teacher.

Efren Villalobos has been in the special education field for more than 20 years, working as a job coach, community-based instructor, academic skills class teacher, and inclusion teacher. Villalobos currently works in a behavior skills class with students who have varying degrees of emotional disorders. He is also a student council advisor at his New Mexico high school, stressing the inclusion of all students. He serves on the board for a local nonprofit, Border Servant Corps, that helps with the transition of migrants and asylum-seekers into the United States.

Foreword

Dr. Alysha Collins
School Psychologist

As a school psychologist who has practiced in Nebraska, Indiana, and now in London, England, I've seen students and their parents/guardians progress through various school systems successfully and amidst challenges. At times, it can be difficult to watch parents struggle to know how to support their teens or to see students become upset because they feel like they are letting their parents down or they didn't get the score they wanted on an important, high-stakes exam. What may be even more discouraging is when parents try to persuade their students into achieving what *they* want or what they think society believes is important. It is also hard to witness students with plans for the future that don't fill them with passion and excitement for what they want their futures to become.

After COVID-19 and witnessing the world shut down, many individuals decided to change the course of their lives and start new jobs, pick up novel hobbies, or move to different places around the globe. It also made me turn to the positive psychology concept of hope, which was the topic of my dissertation and helped guide me to the next chapter of my life. Hope, for me and many others, has been a transformative force that offers the promise of a brighter tomorrow, even in the darkest of times. It has not only inspired me in times of significant, life-changing uncertainty, but it also continues to be a daily mantra during the everyday trials of life.

Hope is important. Sometimes even more important for positive outcomes than grades or assessment scores. Hope has been shown to reduce anxiousness and depression, while also increasing levels of problem-solving, well-being, and effectiveness. Hope also indicates more success in law school than the LSAT for legal scholars. Rooted in belief and possibility, hope empowers individuals to envision a better future and find pathways to their goals. It's the premise that with every challenge there are opportunities for growth and learning, and with each setback there's a chance to build resilience and new ways forward. For a parent, hope can help foster an environment where optimism, support, and encouragement flourish. Hope is truly what all parents should have for their children, regardless of where they are in school or in life.

As your student approaches their* junior year of high school, they have probably already heard some of the following questions by teachers, peers, guidance counselors, or other adults: What college do you want to attend? When are you taking the ACT or SAT? What is your current GPA? Does it correspond with the entry-level requirements at your top university choice? What do you want to study in college? These questions not only put a lot of pressure on a student, but they also make them see only one option after high school. Some students may know what they want to pursue, while others may still be thinking about the next phase. Just because they haven't made a decision yet doesn't mean they are behind.

If your student wants to take the ACT or SAT to go to a four-year university, they should have hope. If your student wants to go into a trade field at a technical school, they should have hope. If your

---

* The pronoun they/them is used in its singular form throughout the book because it is the most practical and inclusive approach.

student wants to work after high school, they should have hope. If your student wants to take a year off to travel, they should have hope. Think of hope as a catalyst for change by helping ignite creativity and fueling aspirations.

It is never too late to provide hope for your student. Not all students progress toward the next chapter in the same direction, and you help them to see opportunities they may not have considered or had the courage to explore. When your student encounters a setback or experiences a period of adversity this year, encourage them to find new ways to approach a challenge. You are a partner in your student's educational journey, providing steady support, guidance, and a nurturing environment for them to make mistakes and still find ways to problem-solve and thrive.

This book provides multiple opinions and suggestions for parents who may or may not have a wealth of knowledge about the 11th-grade adventure. I encourage you to read it from a place of hope, and share that hope with your student. It will help lay a foundation for a future where your teen is equipped with knowledge, resilience, and determination to navigate life's challenges with confidence. If you haven't asked them yet about what lies ahead, a good place to start is, "What hopes do you have for your future, and what steps can you take to get there?"

Introduction

Timothy M. Dove
2011 & 2012 Ohio State Teacher of the Year

This book is for parents, family members, caregivers, siblings, mentors, and any supporters of a soon-to-be 11th grader. Think of each of these chapters as advice from a friendly teacher in your child's school.

For those of you embarking on the experience of having a junior in your family, you'll find loads of information useful to you and your student.

Each contributor to *11th Grade Ready* is a current or former 11th-grade educator who has worked extensively with parents and families of students. These contributors have all been Teachers of the Year, finalists, or otherwise recognized for their abilities. They are experts in the field overall and in the topics of the chapters they penned.

The chapters that follow cover many of the topics that you may be thinking about as your teen enters 11th grade. Beginning with how 11th grade differs from 10th and moving through preparing them for 12th grade, this book will serve as your guide. It will describe what to expect in a variety of areas and things to look for as you navigate your teen's physical, emotional, and academic growth. This book focuses on action items and tips on how to support your student as they start developing their independence. Some information might seem obvious, while other pieces will be eye-opening. Every family is different, and parts of the book will resonate differently with each reader. Any new information can help you plan and engage with your child. That with which you are already familiar should assure you that you are on the right track.

Most chapters give prompts throughout their pages or conclude with a list of conversation starters. In thinking about how to use these lists, consider your student's history, your relationship with them, and other family dynamics. Using open-ended questions is the best way to get information from your student. Not only will having these conversations assist you in supporting your 11th grader, but they will also open new lines of communication that can continue throughout the school year.

This book can be used in different ways. You can focus on the chapters needed, or of interest, based on timing, or you can read it straight through to get a sense of the landscape of 11th grade to spark ideas. This is a transitional year for your teen, as the end of high school is on the horizon. This realization adds another level of anxiety and excitement for the near future. We hope this book helps you navigate the journey.

Chapter 1

HOW IS 11TH GRADE DIFFERENT FROM 10TH GRADE?

Ways to support your student during this transitional year

David Bosso
2012 Connecticut State Teacher of the Year

When Gabriella was a freshman in my world history course, she often struggled to maintain interest and attention, and her work completion was inconsistent. Relative to her peers, Gabriella was academically and socially immature, and these behaviors often caused tension in the classroom. On a number of occasions, I spoke with her privately in an effort to redirect and focus her so that she would be successful in the course and begin to take things seriously. Fast-forward to Gabriella's junior year, when she was enrolled in my sociology course. Gabriella's overall approach and demeanor seemed transformed: She paid attention, expressed interest, remained engaged, took notes, completed her work, and earned excellent grades. Her interactions with her peers in the classroom were positive and productive. She was consistent and determined. Several weeks into the school year, I pulled her aside.

"Gabriella, you are doing a fantastic job! I have to say, though, that this is very different from when you were in my class a couple of years ago. What changed?" Gabriella thought about it for a moment, and replied, "I don't know. I just figured some things out."

Although Gabriella represents a more extreme version of what may transpire in a student's life, the fact is that many students experience noticeable academic and social changes throughout their time in high school. In other instances, personal evolution is perhaps less dramatic and more subtle. It is particularly rewarding when such a metamorphosis is indicative of an increasing sense of awareness, gravitas, and dedication. In Gabriella's case, as with many students as they transition from one grade level to the next, she began to recognize the longer-term implications of decisions she was making. She came to realize that she should begin laying the groundwork for the next phase of her life and her future career. The habits that she was forming could be beneficial or detrimental, and she astutely began to alter her choices, attitudes, and overall approach to school and life.

Freshman year is one of transition and assimilation to a new community and school culture. Initially, many students feel overwhelmed, followed by a period of settling in and becoming acclimated to the new environment. By their sophomore year, students may feel a stronger sense of identity—with their school, peers, and themselves. The unease and anxiety associated with navigating the hallways, remembering locker combinations, and becoming attuned to new norms, expectations, and workloads usually gives way to a sense of comfort and familiarity. Junior year, however, is often characterized by new demands and pressures. Like Gabriella, students begin to get a much more profound appreciation of the weight of their decisions. Coupled with thinking about the years looming on their personal horizon—which, of course, is both exhilarating and perhaps somewhat discomfiting—junior year becomes quite consequential.

Understanding Course Load

One of the most obvious differences between your student's sophomore and junior years is the course load. Many students challenge themselves with more rigorous and demanding courses at the Advanced Placement, International Baccalaureate, or honors levels. The pace of these courses is often faster and concepts may be at a higher level. The workload, in terms of frequency and types of assignments, is heavier. Assignments may be longer, such as a higher number of pages to read or longer written assignments requiring deeper analysis and synthesis of information. There also may be a gradual release of responsibility, in which teachers expect students to take charge of their own learning, time management, and organization. By this point in your student's high school experience, teachers may not be prompting them to take certain notes or reminding students as much about upcoming deadlines. Part of this academic transition means that there is an understanding that students have developed, and perhaps refined, their academic skill set. They may have a repertoire of strategies that they use for note-taking, work completion, and assessment preparation. This is not to say that teachers absolve themselves of any obligation to offer guidance and support. On the contrary, teachers continue to do so, but the manner in which this takes place looks and feels different as students cultivate the necessary skills and dispositions associated with their evolution as learners.

Finding Their Stride

Some students may feel that, in retrospect, their sophomore year was more difficult. For a number of high school students, the adjustment period into a more rigorous high school setting may take some time. Students may feel that the demands of sophomore year relative to their freshman year are more stringent than the ensuing transition to junior year. By junior year, some students may feel that they know what to expect and have fostered the necessary skills and dispositions for academic success, especially given that they now have two years of experience in high school. From a social standpoint, students may experience shifts among their friend groups, perhaps due to the classes in which they are enrolled and/or extracurricular activities in which they participate. This might also be the result of evolving viewpoints, interests, values, and maturity levels, as well as their increasing understanding of demands, expectations, and future academic prospects. After their first two years in high school, students' sense of familiarity, confidence, and belonging—with academics, within the social environment, and with their self-identity—may be stronger.

Considering Electives

In addition to considering enrolling in more challenging courses, students may also choose to register for various elective courses to get a better sense of their interests and potential pursuits beyond high school. Ideally, there will be room in a student's schedule, and electives may be a welcome reprieve from other types of scholarly experiences. Even if there is only a glimmer of interest, it may be valuable to take a course that a student may not otherwise have considered. There is always the possibility that other academic and life demands, such as required courses, jobs, family responsibilities, and the like, might preclude one from having such an academic experience ever again. Furthermore, such courses can provide important groundwork for critical life skills. Courses in fields like technology, the arts, music, personal finance, and culinary arts, for example, may prove to be not only thoroughly enjoyable and memorable, but may also equip students with skills and ideas that they might not have had the chance to explore otherwise.

If possible, a student should also consider having a study hall in their schedule. Some students may have after-school obligations, such as extracurricular activities, employment, or family responsibilities, and having some time during the school day to stay on top of one's coursework may turn out to be vital. Study hall may also be a necessary "brain break" or respite during a busy day. As students' schedules, both in school and out, become increasingly more demanding, a study hall is a block of time to address sundry academic and other tasks.

Balancing Extracurriculars In and Outside of School

Students moving into their junior year may also start thinking about the number of extracurricular and club activities that are offered by their school and beyond. Such activities provide the opportunity to become more involved in community service, learn about potential career interests, and interact with students beyond their close group of friends and classmates. A club may be advised by a teacher or staff member with whom a student may not have interacted, and such individuals may be among the most important adults in the building for certain students, offering advice and insights they might not get in a traditional classroom setting. Such experiences can be an excellent way to bolster one's résumé, particularly as students begin thinking more deeply about their post–high school years. A student's participation in activities beyond the classroom may make a profound difference in their high school career, potentially providing important life lessons, new friendships, lifelong memories, and life-changing experiences.

Starting to Prepare for Post-High School

While students may have taken the PSAT as sophomores as a preliminary assessment, they will take the SAT and/or ACT their junior year. Many students opt to prepare for these assessments with extra practice, and many resources exist, from books to online platforms. Of course, for many students, these assessments are associated with their post–high school plans, and junior year is characterized by increasing interest, and perhaps stress, related to selecting a college or other post-high school occupation. Some students will visit a number of colleges and universities the summer after the completion of their junior year to get a better sense of which institutions they should apply to. Students must realize that, although the significance of their impending decision and the prospect of a major life change can generate anxiety, they are fortunate to even have the option of furthering their education beyond high school. When I talk with students who express their concerns over the school choice they have to make, I tell them that it is a win-win situation—some of the most important people in their life they have yet to meet. They will be going off to college, preparing for a career, building relationships with new people, and having an influence beyond what they may have ever dreamed possible.

Closing Advice

I ran into Gabriella several years later during the summer, and she was doing well. She told me about what she had been up to and the college courses she would be starting in a few weeks. I could not help but mention our conversation from her junior year, when it seemed like she had turned a corner. Although it was not an epiphany or a planned action, Gabriella knew that if she had not become more serious about her efforts and overall attitude toward school, things might have turned out differently for her. While this is not to suggest that her junior year was a completely "make-or-break" situation, this point in high school was crucial for her personal and academic growth. Junior year can be a pivotal moment in your teen's high school experience.

Conversation Starters

- How has high school shaped your personality traits, skill sets, and preparedness for future situations?
- What are some interests, ideas, goals, or aspirations for your post-high school plans? What do you hope to accomplish before graduation?
- What are your areas of academic strengths and areas in need of improvement? In what ways can these traits be an advantage or a challenge?
- Beyond the academic elements of school, what are your priorities, concerns, and interests, and how might these factors contribute to future social, emotional, and academic growth?
- In what ways can I support you throughout the high school experience?
- In what ways do you think my interests, experiences, and perspectives influence your views of school, activities, community involvement, and career?

Chapter 2

HOW IS AN 11TH GRADER DIFFERENT FROM A 10TH GRADER?

What to expect from your 200-month-old

Andrea Sachs
History Teacher, Minnesota

When I meet my U.S. history students at the start of the school year, I always think, "Who are these babies?" Then I remind myself that I am unconsciously comparing my September juniors to the May juniors I said goodbye to the previous spring. That realization always makes me excited for the year ahead, because I know how much my students will grow during the course of two semesters. Years ago, I began summarizing this remarkable growth as the "Magic of Junior Year." Witnessing and supporting that magic is one of the great joys of my career in secondary education. While every student navigates through 11th grade at their own pace and in their own way, it is always thrilling to see virtually all of them evolve into more mature, intentional, and self-directed versions of themselves. One of the best parts of my job is catching glimpses of the amazing adults my students are turning into.

I hope this chapter provides tips on how parents can most effectively support their juniors through this phase of growth and transition. I will also sketch out how juniors themselves—who are, after all, the key stakeholders in this process—typically experience 11th grade. Finally, I will finish up with some tips on how to approach parent-child interactions. My goal is to provide information that will help parents navigate thoughtfully and effectively throughout the year.

The Magic of Junior Year

Each September, my school hosts a back-to-school night, when parents move from classroom to classroom to get 10-minute overviews of their high-schooler's courses. After I preview my U.S. history course, I spend time sharing my thoughts about the Magic of Junior Year. This choice is quite deliberate on my part, because parents play a critical role in supporting and nurturing their student's growth. While it's always best for parents to encourage their student's autonomy, they are by no means passive bystanders. I want my students' parents to begin the year with a sense of excitement and optimism, and I invite them to see me as an ally in the work of supporting, and ultimately launching, their students.

So how do I turn my observations, developed over several decades of working with this age group, into a useful message? First, I address the trepidation that many parents feel as the year begins. Some get a little weepy as they anticipate the major family transitions that follow graduation, while others wonder whether their young adult will be ready for the challenges they will encounter after high school. Whatever is on their mind when they walk into my classroom on back-to-school night, it can feel like a heavy load. Telling parents not to worry would be a pointless endeavor, but I do try to reframe junior year as a dynamic phase that can be a lot of fun to witness. My core advice for parents is to support their students' growth, stay out of their way as much as possible, expect surprises, and enjoy the ride. I remind them that all of us—parents, teachers, and, most of all, the students themselves—are invested in helping these proto-adults grow and evolve.

The Bat Phone

I have found that teamwork among adults is a valuable tool when leveraged carefully. Over the years, I have worked with many parents who encourage their juniors' independence while keeping adult-to-adult "back channels" open. You know your teen better than anyone, I remind parents, and I know high school juniors. So why don't we pool our knowledge and expertise? To emphasize this point, I project a slide with an image of the red Bat Phone from the old *Batman* television show. The Bat Phone reminds parents that they can reach out to me with questions or concerns. (I don't know whether I am Batman or Commissioner Gordon in this scenario.) For example, a parent might want me to know:

- If there are circumstances outside my classroom, such as health or family issues.
- If a junior is experiencing a challenge that might affect how they show up in my classroom.

Having this information doesn't mean that I'm going to pull my students into my office for a heart-to-heart conversation, but it does mean that I can keep an eye out for them and provide encouragement or flexibility as needed.

I also promise them that I will communicate any concerns that I have, such as:

- I am noticing a dramatic change in the student's performance or level of interest in my course.

- I have seen a pattern of avoidant behaviors, like asking for extensions or being absent from class on days when projects or assessments are due.

In other words, support for juniors' burgeoning independence can coexist comfortably with clear, open lines of communication among the adults.

Student Compliance

As familiar as I am with the developmental arc of 11th grade, I am also a committed lifelong learner who is open to challenging my own assumptions and adjusting my actions accordingly. For example, as a veteran teacher, I find that I place less value on student compliance than I once did. Some students are naturally inclined to seek approval from the adults in their lives, while others seem to care much less about what the grownups think. There is absolutely nothing wrong with either tendency. However, my years of experience as a history teacher, as well as a six-year stint as a college counselor, led me to think more broadly about student behaviors. I now find myself taking a more value-neutral approach to the adult-pleasers, the rugged individualists, and those in the middle. It is certainly easier to manage the people pleasers, but I also want them to act on their own behalf without tamping down their preferences. And many of the students who seem immune or resistant to adult advice may just be engaging in age-appropriate testing of boundaries and taking their newfound sense of independence out for a spin. I share these perspectives because they have helped me not just as a classroom teacher, but also during the year when I was parenting my own junior.

The Student Experience

Enough about the adults! What does junior year feel like to the students who experience it? There is certainly a wide variety of experiences, but here are four common themes:

Boost in Status

Juniors often feel a boost in their status now that they are in the second half of high school. At school, the dynamic between adults and students definitely shifts now that they have joined the ranks of the "big kids." Teachers, administrators, and coaches typically move toward a relationship marked less by supervision and more by partnership. This shift shows up in the instructions I give for daily assignments in my history course. Rather than prescribing specific homework routines, I invite my students to experiment with their daily practices—and consult with me if they'd like to—in order to find a method that works for them. Not surprisingly, juniors typically respond well to these subtle shifts and approach adults as allies and mentors.

Ability to Chart Their Own Course

In terms of autonomy and choice, juniors often have more opportunities to chart their own course. They have room in their schedules to take more electives and engage in new ways with academic disciplines and extracurricular activities. Perhaps a student has fulfilled a graduation requirement in one discipline, such as science, and can now take extra courses in another department, like English, or try an elective in a new field. Outside of academics, juniors assume formal or informal leadership roles in clubs and on athletic teams or land a part-time job. These new opportunities give juniors a chance to surprise themselves, clarifying their talents and interests as they test out new roles.

Flexible Social Dynamics

Social dynamics often shift and smooth out during junior year as well. Juniors are typically more comfortable in their own skin and less hyperaware of how others perceive them (or of how they *think* others perceive them). Boundaries between social groups typically become more porous. As adults observing from the sidelines, we often see students crossing social boundaries more readily. I've seen juniors join a new club or audition for a school play for the first time. When I break a class of juniors into small groups for a project or activity, I usually assume that all of my students can work productively with anyone in the class, rather than just their friends.

Awareness of the Future

While juniors move through the year keenly aware that they are "on deck" for their senior year, graduation still feels comfortably far off. Most juniors begin to explore post-high school options, some with great enthusiasm and excitement and others with more worry. This awareness of future changes can provoke a wide range of shifting and overlapping responses, from what I call "anticipatory nostalgia" to unbridled glee to panic. The same junior who weeps at the end of an athletic season as they say goodbye to senior teammates may want to throw a party after completing a challenging required course.

The Parent-Child Relationship

I'd like to end this chapter with a return to the parent-child relationship, offering some advice that reflects both my decades as a classroom teacher and my six-year stint as a college counselor.

Less Helpful Messages

Some parental messages and behaviors, while well-intentioned, tend to be less helpful. I always cringe when parents announce, at the start of their child's junior year, "This is the year that really matters!" Parents often deploy this message in the hope that it will motivate their junior to buckle down, work hard, and generally give their academic life a serious makeover. Unfortunately, this tactic usually just provokes anxiety in their teenager and, potentially, conflict at home. I also encourage parents to avoid the "more is more" trap: more extracurricular activities, as many classes as the school allows, community service, university-level scientific research, and so forth. A jam-packed schedule is more likely to stress your child out than it is to wow a hypothetical college admissions officer.

Helpful Approaches

Fortunately, there are many parental attitudes and interventions that can help foster a junior year marked by growth, connection, and equanimity. Parents can support the Magic of Junior Year by encouraging exploration, staying open to new developments, and refusing to pigeonhole their children. For instance, your student may be excelling in a challenging science elective. That's wonderful! Try to repress the urge to jump ahead in the script and map out their college major and career path. Instead, ask questions about the course, and give your junior a chance to articulate what they are learning and what they find exciting or engaging. When you speak to your junior, try to listen, ask questions, and be as stingy as you can with direct advice.

Early in your child's junior year, have a family conversation about how much of their business gets shared with others. Does the circle of support extend to grandparents, aunts, and uncles, or is it limited to the immediate family? I've seen students get pretty frustrated when parents post private information on social media or share ACT scores while they're waiting in line at Starbucks. This advice gets much more pertinent during senior year, but junior year is a great time to establish norms.

Finally, do your best to make your home a place of rest, support, and connection. How can you help your junior prioritize health and wellness? How can you help them establish healthy patterns in terms of sleep and nutrition? How can you help them find healthy stress-relieving activities and maintain a bit of white space on their calendar?

Closing Advice

Junior year is a transformational phase for parents, too. Be kind to yourself and reach out to your own support network when you need it. I hope your child's junior year is full of growth and magic.

Conversation Starters

- Which circumstances at home would you like me to convey to your teachers if you think they may affect your work?
- If you are going through a tough time this year, who do you imagine turning to for support?
- Do you see yourself as a people pleaser or resistant to adult advice?
- In what ways do you feel your teachers are giving you more independence as a junior?
- In what ways do you feel comfortable crossing social boundaries now that you are a junior?
- Which courses do you feel most excited about this year?

Chapter 3
HOW DOES INCLUSION AND BELONGING HELP MY STUDENT?

How to encourage both in academic and social settings

Efren Villalobos
Special Education Teacher, New Mexico

Close your eyes and go back and remember what it was like to be in school. Better yet...high school! For some, it was the best time of their lives. For others, it may have been the worst. We all worked hard at creating and maintaining relationships, both friendly and intimate, with our peers. We all wanted to feel or be a part of something, to be included and to be in the know. Technology has made the world closer but has managed to separate us in so many other ways. Many teenagers nowadays are struggling to fit in with groups or people who are hundreds or even thousands of miles away. That is a far cry from what many of us went through when we were in high school.

I hope to provide you with a bit of insight into what inclusivity looks like today in high school, particularly for 11th graders who are only a year out from legal adulthood. For many of us teachers, this is the most important year, as testing, grades, and college selection begin to take on a much bigger role in your student's life. They will begin to juggle the importance of school with their social life—and there will be days when you will stand back in shock because you have no idea what they could be thinking. It's okay. You will not be alone. Your student will have a strong support system at school, and they will have teachers who will point them or guide them in the right direction.

As a special education teacher, inclusion is an important part of my objective. When working with students with varying disabilities, I need to help make them feel included in all aspects of school life, both academic and social. They will be preparing to graduate in a couple of years and will need to be productive members of society. I will cover the importance of inclusion in academic and social aspects from the points of view of the special education student and the general education student. You will find that many of the objectives are the same.

The Importance of Academic Inclusion

An inclusive setting in an academic environment is important for various reasons. Here are just five key reasons inclusion is crucial:

It helps to promote diversity and equity. Inclusion ensures that students from diverse backgrounds, including those with different abilities, ethnicities, socioeconomic backgrounds, and learning styles, have equal access to educational opportunities. This promotes equity and diversity, fostering a learning environment that reflects the real-world diversity students will encounter beyond academia.

It enhances learning for all. An inclusive setting provides a variety of perspectives and learning styles, creating a rich and dynamic learning environment. When students with diverse abilities and strengths learn together, they can collaborate and support each other, leading to a more holistic and effective learning experience. This benefits everyone.

It develops empathy and social skills. Inclusion helps students develop empathy and understanding by asking them to interact with individuals who may have different abilities or challenges. This exposure to diversity fosters compassion and tolerance, contributing to the development of strong interpersonal and social skills. These skills are essential for success both within the academic setting and in future professional and personal endeavors.

It prepares students for the real world. Inclusive settings mirror the diversity of society, preparing students for the real world, where they will encounter people with various abilities and backgrounds. Exposure to diversity in the educational environment equips students with the skills needed to navigate and contribute positively to an inclusive society, which helps promote social cohesion and understanding.

It complies with legal and ethical standards. In many countries, there are legal requirements and ethical standards promoting inclusive education. Meeting these standards ensures that educational institutions provide equal opportunities for all students. By fostering inclusion, institutions not only comply with legal mandates, but they also demonstrate a commitment to the principles of fairness, equality, and social justice.

The Importance of Social Inclusion

In a social setting, particularly for 11th-grade students, either abled or disabled, fostering an inclusive environment is crucial for several reasons:

Inclusion helps with social development and peer relationships. Inclusion in a social setting helps students develop strong interpersonal skills and build positive relationships with peers. It provides opportunities for students to interact with individuals from diverse backgrounds, fostering understanding, tolerance, and the ability to collaborate effectively.

Inclusion cultivates a supportive community. An inclusive social setting creates a sense of community and belonging among students. Feeling accepted and supported by peers contributes to positive mental health, reduces feelings of isolation, and enhances overall well-being. This supportive atmosphere is particularly important during adolescence.

Inclusion promotes leadership and collaboration. Inclusion encourages students to take on leadership roles and collaborate with others, regardless of differences. Eleventh graders have the chance to develop teamwork skills, effective communication, and the ability to work with diverse groups. These skills are valuable not only in their current social setting, but also in future academic and professional endeavors.

Inclusion prepares for a diverse society. A socially inclusive environment prepares students for the diversity they will encounter in college, the workforce, and society at large. Exposure to different perspectives, cultures, and identities helps students become more open-minded and adaptable, contributing to their ability to thrive in an increasingly interconnected world.

Inclusion enhances emotional intelligence. Inclusion fosters emotional intelligence by exposing students to a range of emotions and experiences. Navigating diverse social situations helps 11th graders develop empathy, resilience, and the ability to manage interpersonal conflicts. These emotional intelligence skills are essential for building strong, positive relationships throughout their lives.

Real-Life Examples

I would like to share responses to a survey I gave out to my high school's 11th graders. I reached out to everyone, including our most vulnerable populations: our English language learners (ELLs) and special education students. While I wish I could include *all* of the answers from the survey, I have elected to sum them up, as many of them were similar. I will include a quote from a student and then summarize other answers.

1. What does inclusion mean to you, and why do you think it's important in a school community?

    "Inclusion means to me that everyone is included and being included helps to build self-esteem."

    For many students, being a part of something is important to build self-esteem and character. When the students feel included, they feel safe and a part of something that is bigger than themselves. Being included also gives students motivation and school spirit.

2. Can you share an experience where you felt included or excluded and how it impacted you?

    "I feel excluded when my teachers don't speak my language and don't make the attempt to speak to me in my native language. I feel it is only fair that if I have to speak English, they should learn to speak some Spanish." (translated)

    This was a common response from many of our ELLs. Many of them take a developing English course to help them learn English. Often, teachers have endorsements to teach students in other languages, but many do not. Many school districts are requiring their teachers to become endorsed in TESOL (Teaching English to Speakers of Other Languages) to support ELL students.

"Being in an inclusion classroom has helped me get smarter and work harder and is preparing me for life after school."

For context, an inclusion setting in a classroom is when a special education student is placed in a general education classroom, and a special education teacher is in the classroom with the regular education teacher. In a perfect world, both teachers co-teach, and students in the class will not know who the special education and regular education students are; the class should feel like any other "normal" class.

3. Are there specific activities or initiatives you think would help strengthen the sense of belonging for all students in our school?

The most common response from all of those surveyed was for the school to offer more after-school activities and additional sports on top of the traditional football, basketball, etc. Sports teams tend to unite students from many different backgrounds or capabilities.

4. What role do teachers and school staff play in fostering inclusion, and how can they contribute to creating a more inclusive environment?

"Teachers and staff play a really big role. I like how teachers make different groups for students to work with different people."

This was the consensus among all the students. It is important for teachers to set up groups with students with different capabilities so they can work together on a project. The more students work with diverse learners, the more ready they will be for the real world.

5. How can students actively contribute to making their school a place where everyone feels welcome and valued?

All the students surveyed used the same words: Be kind. Be friendly. Be respectful. Be welcoming to others. As the students say, "Say less!"

6. In what ways can technology and social media either help or hinder inclusion among students?

"Responsible social media and technology use is important. Most of us already know how to use social media more than our parents. We just need our parents to supervise us better because it can get out of control."

Most of the students surveyed didn't believe that social media or technology was a problem. They felt most of the problems came from certain individuals who didn't use social media "the right way." Those individuals take advantage of others and give social media a bad name. It isn't until something bad happens that parents begin to pay attention to what is going on with their teen's social media pages.

7. Do you have any advice for the incoming juniors about what it means to be inclusive or how to be inclusive of others?

"Respect everyone despite their ethnicity, their race, or the language they speak. Learn to speak the language of the people you want to be friends with. Don't make fun of them because that could affect the person in a negative way." (translated)

"Be sociable and know as many people as you can so that you can have more friends. Help other people to feel more included." (translated)

"Never lose your spirit and protect your character. You are neither more nor less than anyone else." (translated)

"Stop acting like little kids. Grow up. You will need friends when you graduate."

"Make friends with those around you. Do your best to find any sort of common ground. Do not go around making enemies, because it will only get worse."

"Take care of each other; you are going to need it in the end. Notice what is going on around you and with your friends. You may save someone's life."

Closing Advice

We have all been in those situations, especially in high school, when we were included in things and left out of others. We remember the highs of being included on a sports team and the lows of not being invited to the popular kid's house party. Many students are going through what we went through when we were in high school. Don't be afraid to talk to your child and let them know you remember what it is like. You, too, have been there. Let your child know that they are not alone and you can take the time to talk through those feelings and figure out a way to make it better. Your 11th grader only needs to know that they have your support and your attention through good and bad.

Conversation Starters

- How do you feel about the level of inclusion and diversity in your school? Are there any areas where you think improvements could be made?

- Can you share an experience where you felt truly included and accepted by your peers or teachers? What made that moment stand out to you?

- In your opinion, what steps could the school take to promote a more inclusive environment for students of all backgrounds and abilities?

- Are there any clubs, activities, or initiatives in your school that focus on promoting diversity and inclusion? How do you think they contribute to the overall school community?

- How comfortable do you feel expressing your unique identity, ideas, and perspective in the classroom? Is there anything you think can enhance the overall sense of acceptance among the students?

Chapter 4
DIFFERENT LEARNING STYLES AND ACCOMMODATIONS

How understanding the way your student learns can help them

John Skretta
2017 Nebraska Superintendent of the Year

More than 30 years ago, Howard Gardner articulated a framework for expanding our understanding about different ways of being smart. His groundbreaking work on multiple intelligences in 1993 was followed by his book, *Frames of Mind,* in 2011. The work of Gardner and others helped teachers, students, and parents realize and accept that not all learners learn in the same way or at the same pace. While educational researchers have continued to debate the merits of this theory, it remains useful in helping us understand that some students have a preferred mode for learning information, or "learning style," that reflects a comfort zone with taking in that new information and making sense of it.

Four of these foundational learning styles that have been defined repeatedly and revisited frequently in educational theory and practice are:

- Visual—These students learn best through pictures, photos, and diagrams, and may take in information especially fluidly when it is conveyed in a pictogram or graphic organizer.
- Auditory—These students learn through hearing and the verbal mode; they exhibit strong recall of conversations and information conveyed orally.
- Kinesthetic—These tactile students learn best through physical activity, prioritizing movement when incorporating information, such as in constructing models and using their hands to master content.
- Linguistic—These students learn best through literacy and can be provided text in advance and demonstrate an initial grasp of key concepts; they possess a keen ability to convey main points and supporting ideas in writing.

Differentiation of subject matter and strategy is also known as *responsive* teaching, or teaching that is respectful of the learning styles of individual students. For a learner who knows their preferred learning style, no content is inaccessible if it can be reformulated in a way that works with their aptitude. If you see your high school junior working diligently but struggling, a mismatch of content delivery and learning styles may be at play, and there are a variety of things you can do to help your student overcome this challenge.

Productive Struggle Versus Floundering and Failing

There is a big difference between **productive struggle** and floundering that leads to failure. The former is something that parents should embrace and expect to see in an academically rigorous environment. It should be expected that your junior will struggle at times to synthesize a lot of new information in many different areas (math, science, English, history). Junior year can be daunting because the slate of courses may include advanced mathematics, chemistry or anatomy and physiology in science, and Advanced Placement courses that are offered in the English language arts and social studies realms. Even electives may contain more dual credit courses or Advanced Placement opportunities, such as psychology and economics. In short, junior year can be a lot, even for the best prepared and most capable student. So, some struggling is just going to come with the territory. You are well-equipped to tell if your teen is productively struggling or floundering in a way that could lead to failure.

When things have reached a point where you are witnessing excessive and unproductive struggling, it's time to take action. What are these red flags? They might include:

- Your teen suddenly seems disinterested in or apathetic about coursework that was previously engaging.
- Your teen expresses anger or hostility along the lines of, "This stupid class!" or "The teacher's dumb."
- Your teen consistently complains about a lack of relevance in the course, with statements like, "I'll never use this anyway; what's the point?"

Read on for a number of ways that you can explore if there is a lack of accommodation for learning style differences and how to partner with the school to promote your student's success.

Know Your School's Instructional Model

Most accredited high schools have an instructional model for their school system that is a standardized set of expectations on teaching strategies. There may be standard instructional strategies that your junior's teachers are expected to use with regard to lesson design, classroom management, and formative assessment. If your junior is suddenly struggling in one class or area, it may be helpful to explore with the teacher (and administration when appropriate) whether the full range of instructional strategies are being deployed at the classroom level to help your student. For example, a **formative assessment** functions as a check to see how progress is being made within a chapter or unit of study. A **summative assessment** is intended as a reflection of accomplishment of major learning objectives, usually covers several chapters or units, and has a substantial impact on a course grade. Two important questions to ask your junior are:

1. Are the results of your unit tests indicating that you may have a studying problem in one or more of your classes?

2. Are these unit tests aligning with the content that is being tested on the larger exams?

If your student is performing well on formative assessments but struggling on summative assessments, there is a mismatch somewhere. It could be that your teen is flourishing with a variety of learning styles that are acceptable on formative assessments, but the summative assessment is a standard essay or multiple-choice format exam.

> ### Unidentified Special Learning Needs
>
> It may be possible that your student possesses a genuine disability that interferes with the ability to succeed in a regular classroom environment. They may have a qualifying condition for special education status and/or a 504 plan, which could be put into place during the latter part of your student's high school experience. While it is rare for a student in their junior year to manifest a new condition that qualifies them for special education services, it does occasionally happen. A thorough description of this process exceeds the scope of this chapter, but

> a student who demonstrates qualifying conditions will need the consensus of a multidisciplinary team of educators and a subsequent IEP team to confirm this. When qualification for these services is verified, there are an array of additional protections afforded these students in the learning environment to ensure an equitable educational experience. However, special education should not be considered equivalent to learning styles-based instruction, because special education status is conferred only by an identified disability.

Learn Your School's Policy on Late Work

Sometimes an individual teacher has the decision to accept, deny, or modify a grade if late work is handed in. In many cases, however, a school will have a department-wide or school-based policy in place for the submission of late work for academic credit. If your student is struggling with a mismatch between content delivery and learning style, it may be beneficial to determine whether they can submit assignments and projects within allowable timeline parameters and still receive full credit. Some school districts have moved to accepting late work for full credit through the end of a grading term (quarter or semester), because their focus is on ensuring mastery of the academic objectives and not on the importance of deadlines. Admittedly, mastering the importance of deadlines is an important life skill, but there is a reasonable argument to be made that the course letter grade should be a reflection of demonstration of content mastery *whenever* it occurs within the course. If your junior is struggling and simply needs more time, be sure you know what your teacher and school's policy is on late work.

Find Out if Your School Offers Additional Resources

Many schools offer a Saturday school experience, an after-school study time, or an array of supplemental online resources designed to provide extra credit opportunities for students in core curricular classes to maximize the number of ways in which they can demonstrate meeting key learning objectives. For a student who is struggling in the regular classroom, there may be some online activities that can be completed on your student's own time to help them get up to speed. Demonstrating completion of these tasks can equate to additional points for the teacher's gradebook and a better outcome for your junior.

Does your school have an academic interventionist?

If your junior is struggling in a course and you are stumped as to why, ask whether the school has an academic interventionist, whose role is to provide independent observational input that is nonevaluative but supportive of both the teacher and student to ensure the classroom environment and content meet the student's needs. For schools lacking an academic interventionist or a multitiered systems of support specialist, ask your student's counselor or an administrator if they can informally observe your student in the classroom and provide you and your student with some independent advice and feedback to support better outcomes. See more about indvidualized learning plans in the next chapter.

Does the school have an advisory period?

Many high school schedules include an abbreviated advisor/advisee or mentor/mentee period to provide individual academic assistance to students. Teachers are assigned advisory groups and may have the same group of students over several years, which allows them to foster relationships with a stable peer group. If you have a junior who is struggling, this support period can be helpful because it provides additional opportunities for interaction with a teacher. If your student needs additional help, often these advisory periods will include a short list of resources aggregated by your student's teachers in order to get support in particular classes. If your school offers an advisory period, be sure that your student has a plan for the best use of this resource.

Understand When Differentiation Might Not Be Possible

In their junior and senior years of high school, it may be more common for students to encounter teachers who consider themselves to be subject matter experts first and teachers of children second. These teachers value the acquisition of important content knowledge by students, and they are less interested in demonstrating methodological flexibility in their approach. These teachers may be more reluctant to incorporate a variety of accommodations to ensure each student learns effectively and successfully based on their learning style. For instance, if you have a student who is a strong visual learner and thrives on pictograms and visual representations of key concepts, it could be a challenging AP literature class if the teacher's exclusive focus is on close reading of the text and formal written responses. This may cause friction, because the student's preferred learning style is not reflected in the instructional practices of the teacher. This is a good opportunity for your junior to self-advocate and use some of the strategies on page 34.

Often in high school, college and dual-credit courses are offered to accelerate students' postsecondary aspirations and give them a leg up on pursuing their formal educational journey. These courses are sometimes taught by visiting professors or instructors from the partnering postsecondary institution, whether it's a local community college or a traditional four-year university. In most high schools, however, the dual-credit coursework is taught by a member of the high school faculty who is qualified to teach these college credit classes. These classes provide a more expansive range of learning opportunities for students and ensure that high-performing students do not languish in high school course offerings.

When your student requests alternate pathways for completing assignments in a class like this, it can be challenging. The postsecondary partner institution may have fairly strict expectations regarding student work and be unwilling to vary their formal assessments. This might mean that your student will get high school credit for the course but needs to waive the college credit to succeed in the class. Taking this class gives them a rigorous academic experience without compromising their GPA.

Strategies When Instruction Does Not Align with Your Child's Preferred Learning Style

Communicating directly with the teacher and enlisting the teacher as a partner in education, rather than an obstacle to it, is the best path forward. If you believe your child's junior year could be in jeopardy because a teacher is not meshing well with your student's preferred learning style, equip yourself with some key questions that can enlist help for your student.

- Can my student stay after class? Can my student come in after school or before school to get additional support?
- Does the class offer a layered curriculum? (This means that there are differentiated pathways built into the course so that students are able to pursue a variety of activities, all of which demonstrate comprehension or application of the course's key learning outcomes.)

- Are there supplemental resources or ancillary materials provided in the course curriculum so that my student may be able to better grasp the material and succeed?
- Are there alternate means of demonstrating proficiency in the major objectives of the course? If so, what does my student need to do to indicate interest in pursuing these means?
- Is there any flexibility in assignments for the class? If my student is struggling with completion of a written assignment, is there a way to demonstrate the same learning via a project-based model or a poster that visually displays comprehension and analysis?

The above questions need not be asked in a way that prompts a defensive reply from your junior's teacher. In fact, I am confident you will find that most teachers welcome a dialogue with parents so you can partner to promote your junior's success.

Closing Advice

Accommodating different learning styles and realizing that students bring a vast array of perspectives and backgrounds into any single classroom environment celebrates the diversity of learners and provides a pathway to success for all.

Junior year is one of intense academic rigor for many students, especially those who are aiming to go to college. It is often characterized as a test-heavy year, with state standards and national assessments. This can be very revealing to your junior, who will subsequently know how strong a test taker they are, which should not be confused with being a high-achieving student. Many students possess great intelligence and can demonstrate their learning in different ways, yet they are not excellent test takers. While performing well on standardized assessments has its rewards, it does not define a person and should not deter your student from pursuing their academic goals and interests.

By the conclusion of junior year, your student should emerge with a strong sense of self-identity as a learner. Whatever their preferred learning style, the knowledge of how they learn best empowers them, because students who know their abilities and preferred learning styles have a distinct advantage going forward. As your student approaches the latter part of their junior year, your direct intervention, while well-intended, tends to bring diminishing returns. The sooner you can empower your junior to understand how they learn best, the better their future chances are in education and the workplace.

Chapter 5

LEANING INTO HOMEWORK AND STUDY SKILLS

How can I help my student succeed in the classroom?

Marcy Dovholuk
Assistant Principal, New Hampshire

It's during junior year, unlike other years, that your teen's future hinges directly on what may and may not take place. Eleventh grade is one step closer to the journey that awaits after high school. Your student will be expected to navigate unfamiliar territory and, as a parent, you will be expected to do the same. Together you will be fortunate to embrace the joy and discovery of growth that comes when parent/guardian/child work hand-in-hand.

How your student shows up in school is a choice. And with this choice there are myriad ways in which they may elect to navigate the halls, rooms, fields, and, subsequently, the time outside school. How your student chooses to address in-class work, homework, and other aspects of school is the annual journey this school year. Your teen may feel abundantly ready to move forward alone; however, there will be times that having their parent/guardian squarely by their side will be welcome. It is recognizing these times that is the question.

Constructive Ways to Help with Homework and Study Skills

Perhaps your student has never had to worry about completing homework on time. If so, you are lucky. You may find that this year there will be homework every night of the week and that it will drain your child's stamina. This busy academic year may introduce a newfound appreciation for a dedicated system for homework completion.

It is likely that your teen's school has an online system, which allows you to see grades and assignments. This online system streamlines information between home and school. These online systems are typically quite sensitive, and the grades can change quite a bit in the span of a week, so it's good to check them weekly, not daily. Include your student so they can walk you through the process and give you a sense of their classes/teachers. Perhaps you can come to an agreement with your child about how frequently you will check the online system.

Once you have agreed on a plan for checking grades/class assignments, you might want to come up with a plan for what to do if or when the grades take a dip or assignments are not completed (those dreaded 0s). Sometimes a zero serves to signal to the student and parent that an assignment, quiz, or test is missing. If your child is living in two households, try to abide by the same system in both homes, as it helps communication between child and parents/guardians and, if need be, school administrators/teachers.

Your teen has been in school for years at this point and should welcome the opportunity to communicate with teachers, but not all students embrace this opportunity. As the need arises, email is usually the best way to communicate. You should encourage your teen to write to their teacher about questions/concerns. You might ask that they copy you on the email, which is a good way to be kept in the loop. If you have questions/concerns, you should also feel free to follow up directly with the teacher of record. Many parents/guardians hold off, with the belief that their teen is now of the age that they should be able to do school on their own. Please remember that your child still needs support.

You might relay to the teachers on back-to-school night, or via an intro email at the start of the school year, that you would like to support your student, and—while you hope that they are acting on their own behalf—you are also looking out for their best interests, so you will email from time to time to check in and will communicate directly if there is an issue or concern. Missing assignments or low grades may warrant an email to the teacher. If your student prefers you not contact their teacher, you might ask them to do so and cc you on the email. However, parent contact is important if you feel there is something that is not going well. Being proactive is welcome. Most schools mandate a speedy reply to any parent who reaches out to the school in any fashion.

What if My Student is Falling Behind?

If your teen has fallen behind, do not waste time thinking it will improve without intervention. This is a busy school year, and things have a way of slipping by unnoticed. If you have been checking the online system, you will be aware of any potential issues. You should also celebrate what is working well to build on a positive note, as well as create a focus on what needs improvement.

A good way to support your teen without removing their sense of agency might be to schedule a check-in once a week or every other week. It need not be long, perhaps 15 minutes to take a look at the online platform together. This will encourage conversation about what your student is learning/doing at school without having to ask a lot of intrusive questions. The information available online will allow your teen to share what is going well and perhaps what they feel isn't going well. This will allow for communication that they will hopefully in time lead. When they have shared with you a piece of what is current, you might ask one or two questions or share supportive comments. Here are a few conversation starters that may help you have this sort of conversation with your teen:

- Begin with positive comments: "You've been working diligently on _____."
- "You did it! That project/homework was tough, but you persevered."
- "What are you learning in _____ class now? What are you curious about?"
- "What have you noticed about your _____ class that you find interesting?"
- "How have you been developing your _____ skills in _____?"

If your teen is to take ownership of their learning, they will need your support and encouragement. There are many options these days for online work and submissions. For instance, Google Classroom is one platform for you to view with your student. Perhaps they could decide on one piece of work they would like to share with you. Most schools require submission of work online—things like writing assignments, lab reports, photography work, logs of activity from PE—so all of your teen's work should be found here. Grade 11 is a tricky year in that students are set on a course to independence, but they still need your support and help, even if they reject it outwardly.

To help your teen through a difficult class/unit of study/teacher relationship, you might incorporate some of the following strategies:

- Ask your teen for ways you can help. Suggesting that they have to spend a bit more time and attention on schoolwork is not always welcome.

- Give concrete examples of what might help instead of saying, "Just try your best" or "It's easy."

- Encourage your teen to try the first problem to see how it goes, and offer help along the way.

- Ask your teen what questions they have about the problem(s) at hand.

What If I Notice My Teen Has Challenges Learning?

Your student will likely face challenges at some point during the school year. Perhaps it is in a subject area that isn't as "easy" as some of their other subjects, or perhaps the teacher or classroom setting is not conducive to learning. Identifying the source of the challenge is important. If your teen is voicing concerns, you might ask if they have contacted their teacher. If they have and things are still challenging, then perhaps a call to the teacher is warranted. Your teen's teacher will likely be happy to hear from you. Often a parent who ventures to connect with a teacher will be surprised by the details regarding their teen that the teacher volunteers. We are always modeling for our teens the way to approach problems/concerns, so forge ahead with positivity and promise. You might email the teacher and ask about a good time to connect by phone. Nuances can easily be lost via email, so a phone call, albeit a bit more difficult to schedule, is well worth the effort.

If your student has a 504 plan or individualized education plan (IEP) then you might contact their school counselor or case manager to inquire. If your teen does not have a 504 plan and you feel a closer look at the challenges your student is facing is necessary, and your teen has a diagnosis such as ADHD, you may refer them for Section 504 eligibility. There is a clear process for this, and each school has a designated person who coordinates it. Schools orchestrate 504 plans differently, as some have 504 plan coordinators and other schools have counselors or assistant principals oversee these plans. There is also a process for special education if it appears your teen is in need of individualized instruction as a result of a suspected disability.

If neither of these seem to be a concern, then a teacher/school counselor call, email, or parent meeting may be needed to figure out what is causing the challenge and how your student might move forward.

What If My Student Needs Extra Help in the Classroom or in General?

If your teen is in need of extra help but it doesn't reach the level of a 504 plan or IEP, perhaps a peer tutor, an adult tutor, or the classroom teacher would suffice.

Sometimes organizational challenges get in the way of productivity in and out of the classroom. By grade 11, most students have found a system that works for them, but in many cases their system can be improved upon. That is, their school bag or backpack may be messy or unorganized and their notebooks may need to be spruced up. Cleaning up one's belongings and checking to be sure one has all the necessary supplies is important. You might schedule it as part of a quarterly review process.

The best sources of information are your student and their school counselor. Setting aside time to discuss concerns about progress can be very helpful. Because this is a critical year, it is never a bad idea to ask for a student/parent meeting. If not the school counselor, you might start with another adult in the school your teen trusts or with whom they have rapport. This school year is inherently full of challenges and, often, uncertainty about the future. One way to help your teen is to validate their feelings. Validation improves communication, trust, and resilience—all of which your teen needs this year and as they move toward independence.

Closing Advice

In this critical year, you should strive to keep communication at the forefront, both with your student and the school. Hopefully you already have a good connection with the school counselor or assistant principal or perhaps a school social worker. If not, this is a good time to connect. If you focus on validating what your teen is feeling—instead of trying to "fix" whatever the concern may be—it should lead to productive discussions and potential planning for the near and distant future with your young adult. The goal is independence, and the road your 11th grader is on right now is paving the way, with your help and support. One can't say enough about positive reinforcement, which serves to validate your student's belief in their abilities and enhance their self-esteem.

Above all, your teen needs you to be their parent/advocate/overall helper and one who offers encouragement and love. Your passion and care toward this end will go a long way in modeling and helping your teen excel. Your teen will remember how you reacted as you navigated this critical school year. Your positive reaction to struggles and joy will be something they always remember and will serve to provide a lifelong model.

Conversation Starters

- What do you find inherently joyful about learning?
- What do you wish you could do to show those around you who you really are?
- What would you like to do if you could do anything you wanted to do? Why?
- Do you know anyone who is working toward a goal or struggling with a challenge? How do you think they keep going in the face of adversity?

Chapter 6

MOTIVATING HIGH SCHOOL STUDENTS AND OVERCOMING PROCRASTINATION

How to help your teen avoid procrastination

Jillian Huber
ELA High School Teacher, Illinois

"Can I finish this game?"

"SAT Prep is too boring and overwhelming! There is no point in doing this."

"I have to finish watching game film for Coach."

"My job called me into work because they are short-staffed."

"This assignment is so difficult and time-consuming. Can I just take my late?"

"How long does this essay have to be? I don't think I am going to get it done."

"I will never need to know this after high school."

These are all exact quotes from students in my study hall and English classroom. How often do you, as a parent, hear a phrase or a question like this that leads to procrastination in your teen? Do you wish you could motivate your child in meaningful ways in their academic life?

Reducing Procrastination

Procrastination: a word well-known to most 11th-grade students! Whether it is at home or school, most students this age know how to procrastinate, especially with schoolwork (and chores). Our job as parents and educators is to find out how each student can be motivated to do their work and do it to the best of their ability. By procrastinating and working under time crunches, a student can't do their best work. It is important to develop motivation and non-delaying tactics to become academically successful, which will translate to other facets of life and play a role in their future. High school students meet many challenges daily. Academics, extracurriculars, jobs, test prep, future college or career decisions, and social media demand their attention. Parents and educators can suggest strategies to help students overcome procrastination and become motivated, helping these young adults this year and in years to come.

High school students tend to procrastinate, delay, or postpone many times because they are distracted by something more intriguing to them, like gaming, social media, or hanging out with friends. They do not think about what will happen if they end up in a hurry to get schoolwork or other jobs done. Many times, students will say that they are overwhelmed and feeling anxious about their to-do lists. You can help them realize that if they work on not procrastinating, it will lead to less anxiety and overwhelming feelings. The key to starting these conversations is finding the root cause of the procrastination.

Here is a list of questions you could ask your child when they are procrastinating:

- Are you feeling overwhelmed or anxious about this assignment? How may I help?
- May I help you become more organized to get this assignment done?
- What kind of distractions can you reduce so you can get this assignment done?
- May we make a schedule for this and stick to it?
- Can we break the task into smaller chunk, so it is less overwhelming?

Encouraging Time Management

A useful strategy to instill in any student, but especially for an upperclassman in high school, is time management. Most teachers and classes have lesson plans and assignments done at least a week in advance, some longer. This is a great time to help your child work on ways to effectively master time-management skills. To overcome procrastination, they should use a planner and make a timeline or calendar. These will become crucial tools that could be used in the future, as well as now.

I provide a homework board in my classroom that gives a snapshot of the whole week and what we will be doing in each class. I also post this on Google Classroom weekly. My students know that on Monday morning, I also recommend they write down in their planner what will be happening for the week as an extra reminder. This gives them the chance to look at their personal weekly calendar for extracurricular activities and jobs and prioritize the assignments and projects in order of importance. For long-term assignments, a monthly calendar works best. If I assign students a novel and give them a due date that is a month out, I also hand them a blank calendar. They are in charge of filling out the number of pages they need to read per day and how long they will allow for reading those pages to finish by the due date. I have also done this for large group assignments so that parts can be assigned to each student in the group on a particular day. I find that paper copies work best for this, but an online calendar may work better for some students.

Here are some strategies I have noticed that can help time management:

- Sticky notes arranged as a timeline that can be crumpled and thrown away when tasks are finished (and moved around if deadlines change)
- A shared app or calendar to help increase accountability
- A color-coded system of tracking different activities in a planner on a whiteboard

Providing Structured Space for the Student's Learning Style

Teenagers need to be free from as many distractions as possible while working on schoolwork. In my classroom, it is easy to see that some students work better in certain environments. Some need to work physically closer to me to stay on task. Others may need to work away from their peers with headphones on to get into the zone. A few of my students need to be close to peers to bounce ideas off them because they need that support. At times, I ask students to go work silently with their counselor or in another teacher's room that is empty. As parents and educators, we must find what sort of structured environment works for our teens. At home, you may need a dedicated space for your teen that will minimize distractions and facilitate the style of learning that your student needs. In my home, we have a "homework center" created during COVID-19. There is a space for each of my children.

During the past few years, I have noticed that my older children tend to stay in the kitchen, usually where I am, if they need help with a subject but then retreat to their rooms when they can work on something individually so they can focus better. Having their own dedicated space and knowing that their teachers and parents are helping them succeed in these ways leads to their motivation.

Other things to consider in the workspace:

- Should there be music or not? If so, what will be the rules around playing it?
- Should the space be a phone-free zone?
- Are supplies readily available (e.g., pencils, erasers, pencil sharpener, scissors, glue, tape, calculator, laptop charger)?
- Do other family members respect the space as a homework zone?

Inspiring Motivation

How do you motivate teenagers to do schoolwork when they could be watching TikTok or gaming with their friends? Most days, this is an almost impossible task. This is something that takes work on the parents' and educators' parts. One thing that we can both focus on is encouraging intrinsic motivation—the incentive for engaging in a behavior or completing a task is performing the task itself. The upperclassman years in high school are a great time to give students more responsibility for their learning, academic grades, and future plans. After having taught your student to keep up with tasks and time-management skills, you can now turn over a little responsibility to the student to get the rest done. By cultivating a sense of accomplishment through progress tracking, you can now encourage your student to find satisfaction in their work and celebrate the little victories they have accomplished. At this point, your student will have to learn what intrinsic motivation is and how to use this to meet their future goals. Your child's junior year in high school is really when future goals start to become important.

Here are some questions you could ask your child if they are struggling:

- How do you feel when you successfully complete a task?
- What makes you want to complete a task and do it well?
- What would you like your life to look like in the next five years?
- What can you do now to make your future goals possible?
- Could I help you brainstorm some ideas about how to motivate yourself to work toward your future goals? (See the next section for tips.)

What Current 11th Graders Find Motivating

When I asked some of my current juniors what motivates them, they had great responses, many of them being extrinsic motivators, which is motivation that is driven by external rewards. These might be great discussion ideas when covering motivation with your child.

"We should get grades/points for our work."

"Extra-credit opportunities should be offered."

"Participation points are helpful for some assignments."

"This answer just depends on the student's home life. I used to have a horrible home life down in Texas, and I never wanted to do my homework. I think teachers need to look out for certain patterns in students so they can help anyone who needs help where gaining motivation at home is concerned. Bad home life does not equal motivation at home. They might need someone to support them instead of yelling at them."

"A quiet and clean space to be left alone with no distractions."

"Teachers who are willing to work with their students' athletics schedules help us become motivated to complete assignments because we see they care about our lives outside of academics."

"Food reward!"

"I think that eligibility and good grades should be motivation enough."

"Give less homework and focus more on giving assignments that are truly helpful to what we are learning."

"Knowing how much we will have to do that week. We need to be motivated and know how much time we will have to spend working on homework. I also feel teachers should look at what students have going on each week/night. For example, I felt we had the most amount of homework during homecoming week. This was the opposite of motivating."

"Positive reinforcement and verbal encouragement are very motivating."

"Knowing that if we turn in our homework and get good grades, we have a higher chance of getting into a good college."

"It is motivating when teachers push us to try to finish work in the school building, encouraging us to use time more wisely."

Closing Advice

Now is the time to deepen communication lines about procrastination and motivation with your 11th grader. Your child must know that they can communicate with you, their teachers, coaches, and counselors. We are all here to help them reach their future goals, which are coming up fast for some of them. The ACT and SAT will be taken soon. Applications for colleges and apprenticeship placements will be completed. Every student will have a different idea of what their future will look like, but now is the time to really start down that road. Junior year can be very difficult for some students. They need daily reminders and encouraging adults in their corner. There will be times when they are overwhelmed, but if we all help give them the tools to prevent procrastination and find intrinsic and extrinsic motivation, they will be ready for whatever life, or 11th grade, throws their way!

To help your teen put forth their best efforts for their goals, you can help them:

- Reduce distractions.
- Talk about how to recognize and overcome procrastination.
- Instill time-management skills in their weekly routine.
- Find what motivates them.
- Look toward the future.
- Keep communication open with you, their teachers, their coaches, their bosses, and their counselors.
- Encourage them daily in some way.

Chapter 7
REALITY BITES

How to overcome academic hurdles
and prep for high-stakes exams

Heidi Edwards
Physical Science and AP Biology Teacher, Ohio

Junior year, it hits: the reality of starting to make those first decisions about life after high school. Our students are encouraged to make life decisions about trade programs, associate degrees, entering the workforce, gap years, the military, and four-year college programs while they are still just trying to survive high school. Students begin to realize that the grades they have been accumulating during the past two years of high school are either helping them or providing a bit of pressure to do better. This is also the year when most schools offer more AP classes, as well as College Credit Plus courses or dual-enrollment programs. From my experience having taught all grades at the high school level, this is also the point in their education where there is a transformation in their coursework from just rote memory to application and higher thinking skills. This is a challenge and a change in learning that students truly struggle with. For the first time, how students have always studied isn't necessarily working for them, and they may be deficient in adapting and learning new skills to prepare for whatever their level of coursework might be. Students are also challenging themselves with numerous courses that require additional time investments for success.

Hurdles in the Classroom

While teaching Advanced Placement biology to juniors and seniors, I've noticed that a portion of my students have never really had to try "hard" in their previous courses. They could listen to and complete the work without much effort, not having to study much but still meeting success. While some students are capable of learning as they always have as the courses become more advanced and the content becomes more complex, many students have to learn new approaches for how to study. Typically, after their first test in AP biology, students wonder if they can handle the content, and they are devastated if they receive below an A. In their eyes, anything less than acing the test is a failure. I hear how they have "failed" and aren't "good" at biology, when they are far from failing and far from not being able to handle the coursework. The first test is a great indicator of the amount of work that will be required for success in a course. It is sometimes also the trickiest to prepare for, because they are seeing the structure and format for the first time. What students don't realize in the scheme of school is that learning is a growth process. They aren't always patient with their own personal growth and, to be truthful, parents sometimes forget this as well. So how do you help a student who is struggling in a course and sees themself as unsuccessful?

Setting the Stage

Teachers of upper courses are aware of the challenges these students will face and come to expect these hurdles to pop up during the course of the year. Throughout all academic disciplines, the approach to teaching will vary, but teachers want to see their students succeed. Ideally, each classroom creates a unique culture that will differentiate the needs of the learners when it comes to the content being taught. Part of the learning experience is to be in an environment where the students can take academic risks but still feel supported and provided with a safety net to catch them as they learn. As students are learning how to learn, they will be challenged to stretch themselves not just for success in a given class, but also for success in their future path, wherever that path may lead them. So how is a supportive learning environment created? Let's look at some examples when things seem to go wrong and how those challenges can be developed into a learning experience for growth.

Questioning

What if a student answers a question wrong in class? Students may feel that the eyes of their peers are upon them and they are being judged, but in reality we all answer questions wrong at some point. The first point to note and emphasize with your student is that questions allow the teacher a means to gauge where students are with understanding the content. I ask questions throughout the class period and have students answer and then, as a class, we build on that first answer until we are satisfied that we have crafted a complete answer. This technique gives all students the opportunity to contribute and provides a way to understand why an answer may not be correct or complete and to grow our understanding together. Questioning is a tool which can be used in a number of ways, so many times student comfort comes down to the culture and atmosphere of the classroom. Hopefully, most classrooms are structured to encourage students to take risks and even be vulnerable in order to improve their learning experience. When answering a question, your answer is limited to the knowledge that you possess at that moment; with more knowledge, you will be able to better develop that answer.

Missing Assignments

Missing assignments are another hurdle to success and one that parents can be more involved in assisting with. Missing assignments typically come down to time management or feeling overwhelmed.

First, let's look at your student's schedule. You know your student best and teachers recognize that parents want the best for their kids. Take a moment to truly look at your student's entire life: extracurriculars, academic load, job, and family commitments and structure. What can your junior realistically balance on their plate? What are their true interests? Is it better to take challenging courses in areas of interest instead of just across the board? How does your student handle stress, and what anxieties do grades and courses add to their life? In discussing these questions honestly as a family, you can help guide your student to a schedule that is appropriate.

The second piece to missing assignments is your student's time-management ability. With higher demands on learning more independently and at a higher level of thinking, a different time commitment is necessary for success. I often see students struggle to keep up with their extracurriculars and schoolwork. One of the worst pitfalls that I see in teaching is the lack of time spent outside class in preparation for the next day.

So how does a teenage brain solve the problem? They try to do that homework in the class period before it is due so that it is completed and turned in on time. What they don't realize in the moment is that yes, they completed the assignment, but they are now behind or missing content in the class in which they were sitting when they completed it. This evolves into a vicious cycle that quickly impacts all of their courses. This is also the scenario where many students will resort to copying or cheating in order to meet a deadline. The anxiety of always being behind creates a mental hurdle to learning and leads to typically lower grades and academic disappointment.

So, how do you assist your student? Check in with them. Take the temperature of their stress level—ask how they are handling their coursework. Even though it is hard to do with a teen, setting boundaries is much appreciated, even if your student might not thank you in the moment.

Work to develop and model a schedule that will give them the time needed to successfully complete their assignments while keeping up with their other commitments. Students should be the ones doing the work but model what time management looks like. Encourage your student to talk with their teachers and to gain insight and tips on how to manage their studies. This should be on the student to make those teacher connections, not the parent, as tempting as that might be.

Students need to work on these skills of independence in order to thrive in life, which is the larger goal of parenting and education.

Failed Test

Failing a quiz or test happens. An evaluation is a measure of learning on that day at that time. If your student fails a test, it is a great idea to open a conversation—they need to see you as a partner and not be fearful of consequences.

From the school side, teachers will often pull students aside and talk with them about the evaluation. I offer review sessions, reach out to students who I see struggling with content, and try to assist with additional resources prior to an evaluation. Every teacher will have different policies on grading and test corrections or optional retakes. Each class is structured differently, and it is on your student to understand the opportunities for them to continue their learning and improve their evaluation scores. Making test corrections or reviewing incorrect answers, even if those are not awarded points, are a great investment of time to better understand test structure and wording.

Building off that understanding will lay the groundwork for better performance in the future.

Helping Your Student at Home

Take advantage of any opportunity to meet your student's teachers during open houses or other school events. Let them put a face to your name and associate you with your student. Open houses or curriculum nights are great opportunities to interact with teachers and ask about course syllabi, classroom setup, and expectations for success in the course. By opening a line of communication at the start of the year, you will have a connection to work with the teachers as needed during the year. You might ask:

- Where have you seen students have difficulty in your course?
- What supplemental resources might you recommend to support my student?
- What do you do if you see a student struggling with the content?
- What opportunities do you provide for students to relearn or reengage with content?

Once you have the answers to these questions, you will begin to have a vision for the course and student expectations. If your student is struggling, encourage them to reach out to their teacher. Juniors in high school should be working on initiating contact with their teachers for extra support and questions. If you are worried that perhaps your student is not reaching out for help, have them email the teacher and copy you. This puts onus on the student, teaching them to advocate for themselves and to communicate appropriately with adults.

Standardized Tests

During junior year, students are taking multiple tests, whether it be state-level testing, Advanced Placement or International Baccalaureate tests, or national exams such as the ACT or SAT. These all carry high stakes because they can impact future paths for your student. Many schools and teachers of tested subjects will teach students the structure of the test, because, like learning a play before a big game, learning the format of a test helps you understand how to approach it. Many programs also offer online and in-person testing courses for students to practice. These are all excellent tools, but remember that this, too, can be overwhelming. Be aware of the testing opportunities and educate yourself about what tests are necessary for your student's future pursuits.

I have seen students crumble under the pressure that is placed on them to perform on these tests, so be cautious about how you handle these testing situations with your own student. Be their cheerleader and supporter in the testing process. Listen to your student about what their needs are in this process and what they think will best support these needs. Tap into the guidance department at your student's school as a terrific source of information and support.

Closing Advice

Junior year is a time of high stress but also high rewards for you and your student. Take the time to breathe, embrace their successes, and take their hurdles in stride. Every classroom situation or test score may not be what your student desires, but remember that every experience is one in which they can learn and grow. Remind them to use the resources available, including teachers, counselors, and friends for support, but teach them to advocate for themselves to get the help that they need.

Conversation Starters

- How are you studying to prepare for your test? What seems to work and what isn't working for you?

- What support(s) do you feel you need to be successful in ___ class?

- What class structures are in place to allow you to continue to learn the content that you struggled with, even after an exam?

- What are your stressors and is there anything the adults in your life can do to assist you with them?

- Give an example of a time when you felt academic stress; do you know how you could work to decrease that stress?

- Do you feel that your effort going into a class is reflected in your grade coming out of the class?

Chapter 8

WHY CAN'T MY TEEN GET ALONG WITH THEIR TEACHERS?

Scripts and strategies to support your student

Al Rabanera
Algebra Teacher, California

"Please put away your phone, Chad. Chad, did you hear me? Hello. Did you hear me? Chad."

Chad rolls his eyes, pretending that he does not hear me, and continues to play his mobile video game as I move closer to his desk.

"Chad. I'm going to need you to put your phone away to focus on the lesson. Can you hear me?"

Chad continues to ignore me and focuses more intently on his cell phone.

"Chad. Go ahead and give me your cell phone."

Chad slips his phone into his pocket and shouts, "What? I put my phone away. What else do you want?"

Conversations like these hamper student-teacher relationships. Thankfully, these types of interactions are now few and far between for me, because over the years I have learned strategies and approaches to de-escalate situations. By leveraging the relationships that I have cultivated with students, I try to refocus on the lesson for the day rather than emotionally reacting to a situation to create a power struggle with the class as an audience. But early in my career, that was not always the case. I would often react to situations without being mindful of the outside factors that may have contributed to a situation.

You will likely first hear your student's side of the story and not understand what transpired leading up to the encounter. To really understand the situation, have a conversation with your student and focus on *listening* rather than just waiting to weigh in and provide comments. Here are some questions to start a restorative conversation:

- What is the play-by-play of what happened?
- What were you thinking of at the time?
- What have you thought about it since?
- Who has been affected and in what way? How could things have been done differently?
- What do you think needs to happen next?

Fight-Flight-Freeze Response

In situations like the one that was described with Chad, a reaction to stress causes a response known as fight-flight-or-freeze. When emotions run high, cortisol floods the prefrontal cortex of the brain, limiting the executive functions that are important for higher-order cognitive skills, which help with goal-directed thoughts and actions.

When logical reasoning becomes limited, the brain signals the body to give a fight-flight-or-freeze response. The fight-flight-or-freeze response is not a conscious decision but one triggered by psychological fears and a built-in defense mechanism. It is involuntary and how the body responds to perceived threats involving physiological changes that help someone prepare to:

- Fight: to take action to eliminate the danger
- Flight: to escape from the danger
- Freeze: to become immobile in the face of the danger

Being aware of the fight-flight-or-freeze response is important because it means your student has become dysregulated, or "flipped their lid." For your student to regulate their emotions, it may take some time for them to calm down and refocus. Teaching your student coping strategies will lessen the time it takes to regulate their emotions and access higher-order cognitive skills. At times, a misunderstanding of a situation leads to either the student or teacher (or both) leaving a situation with a feeling of resentment that trickles down into their ongoing relationship.

What can you do to help? The first step is to teach your student to identify and recognize when they are having a fight-flight-or-freeze response to a situation. The next step is to provide your student with coping strategies to mitigate their stress or anxiety, such as:

- Moving to a safe place that feels less threatening or overwhelming
- Slowing down their breathing to reverse the stress response
- Moving around, if they are feeling restless or agitated
- Seeking social support by reaching out to a friend or trusted teacher

Responding Versus Reacting

It is difficult to hear that your student is having challenges at school, especially with their teacher. You may need to intervene to help your student take the steps to begin restoring the student-teacher relationship. These challenges provide opportunities for your student to learn to navigate the way to a resolution. As a parent, one of the first things to do is be an active listener so that your teen feels like they are being heard. It is important to give your teen space to give their account of the situation so they know their feelings are being validated.

The interaction with Chad is an example of an interaction that may have both the student and teacher *reacting* rather than *responding*. A reaction is typically a quick emotional decision without much thought, often tense and aggressive. A response, on the other hand, is a conscious effort to take a step back to review the situation, be more thoughtful, and attempt to consider the available solutions. To move a challenging student-teacher relationship forward, **intentional communication** is the key.

Teach your teen strategies to help them regulate their emotions, especially during tense and stressful situations, so they are able to make more logical decisions about how to respond rather than react. Suggest they:

- Take a pause.
- Gain awareness of what has happened.
- Consider possible responses.
- Ask: What do you think would be the consequences, intended and unintended?

Communication is Key

When situations like the example with Chad happen in a classroom, more than likely you will not become aware of it. This type of quick interaction is one of many that the teacher manages throughout the day and may not reach the threshold to inform a parent. You are even less likely to hear about your teen becoming dysregulated in class from your student. From my experience, situations like these are taken care of between the teacher and the student quickly and relatively easily. However, when the situation escalates because of either a student's or teacher's reaction, rather than a response, the student may have to participate in an intervention to review strategies to mitigate continued behaviors. When interventions are used as a method to change behavior, you will most likely be contacted.

When you do receive that phone call, I'm imagining your first thoughts will be:

1. Is my student okay?
2. What led up to the incident?
3. What was the resolution that either the teacher or the school found for my student's action and reaction?

Listen to what the educator has to say and be willing to provide recommendations about how to address the behavior. You might ask:

- How can I check on the well-being of my student?
- What are both sides (student version/teacher version) of the story?
- How did each side (student/teacher) react and/or respond?
- What can be done differently next time?

From my experience, the best way to get in front of any miscommunication from either the parent's perspective or the teacher's perspective (or both!) is to reach out to the educators at your student's school, including teachers, counselors, and administrators, to develop a rapport that you can access when challenges arise. Communication is a two-way street, and the more often that communication happens, the more informed parents and educators are, which helps support students. Here are some simple strategies that can be used to begin developing rapport with the educators at your student's school:

- Send an email to introduce yourself.
- Attend school functions and introduce yourself.
- Review your student's academic progress early and often.
- Volunteer to serve on a school committee.
- Ask questions when something is unclear or confusing.

Closing Advice

From conversations with students about their experiences with challenging student-teacher relationships, and from my own experiences as a teacher, a strategy that I use is to share my story with students so they can connect with me. And I try to understand why a student could become dysregulated. I am also mindful to not take a student's reaction personally because, often, the student is using the space in my classroom as a place to release their frustrations from stressful situations that happened outside my classroom.

From a teacher's perspective, the steps to mitigating a challenging student-teacher relationship are:

1. Recognize and be able to name what is happening.

2. Communicate what happened.

3. Identify what the next steps are to move forward with restoring the relationship.

From a parent's perspective, think about how closely you can identify with the situation above and how you can use parent-directed interventions. Use these questions to help organize your thoughts:

- How often are you checking in with your student?
- How are you able to know when your student has become dysregulated?
- What are strategies you can use to help your student regulate their emotions?

Chapter 9

BUILDING POSITIVE STUDENT-TEACHER RELATIONSHIPS

How to navigate conflict and solicit good letters of recommendation

John Skretta
2017 Nebraska Superintendent of the Year

By the time students are juniors, they are exhibiting greater independence and shouldering a greater responsibility for keeping their relationships with teachers positive. It's not always easy, but helping your junior effectively manage those challenging relationships also prepares them for a lifetime of success by ensuring they have the social awareness and confidence to do this when they achieve full adulthood and are living independently.

Throughout this chapter, I will focus on a variety of means and methods for maintaining positive and productive relationships with teachers. This can be easier said than done. As students go through the latter years of high school, they are achieving developmental milestones, acquiring greater independence, and building their own friendship groups. For the most part, these are things that parents get the gift of observing and taking pride in for their children. Witnessing the personal development and growing independence of a high school junior as they start preparing for the postsecondary world of higher education and/or the workforce is rewarding for parents who have invested so much effort in helping their teen get to this crucial point.

Juniors in high school can be quick to formulate their own opinions about the likability of their teachers and the relevance of the content being taught by them. Even with positive and trusting relationships on the home front, parents who are inquiring about how school is going may find it harder to break through their junior's shrugs, noncommittal replies, and one-word answers like "fine."

The Crucial Role and Impact of the Classroom Teacher

As a lifelong educator and parent of four boys, I remain steadfast in my belief that teachers must conduct proactive outreach with students and parents, establish rapport with all students, and strive to foster positive relationships with all students. The best teachers are excellent communicators with both students and parents and offer a high degree of transparency about learning objectives and course timelines. This information may be accessible to parents via a learning management system, such as Canvas or Google Classroom, or through the teacher's page on the school website. Teachers who are proactive communicators will also send periodic updates to both students and parents via email that describe any major looming project/assignment deadlines and identify the key tasks to be accomplished.

Master teachers possess excellent subject matter knowledge and deploy a wide range of instructional strategies from their teaching tool kits, but that's not all: They never forget that maintaining a productive classroom environment and ensuring the best learner outcome is also fundamental and a function of positive relationships. Great teachers know and dignify their students as individuals, and both encourage and challenge them to meet their academic and extracurricular goals. They cheer students on and appropriately challenge them to optimize their potential and help them pursue their dreams. However, situations vary and relationships with teachers can also be challenging, strained, and sometimes even contentious. Acknowledging this reality empowers parents to take action appropriately when things are challenging, while also helping students effectively navigate the difficult circumstance of being in a classroom with a teacher whom they don't like or whom they suspect does not like them.

It is very important that you have consistent and ongoing communication with your student about their academic progress and that you are routinely monitoring it by accessing the parent portal or electronic gradebook used by your district. This way, you have a sound awareness of progress to date for your teen if a grading issue or conflict with a teacher surfaces.

How Do I Help Manage the Situation When My Junior Does Not Like or Is Not Motivated by Their Teacher?

Over years of formal education, almost any student will occasionally encounter teachers with whom they just don't forge a strong personal bond or, worse, intensely dislike. This can be for a wide variety of reasons and, depending upon the maturity level and intrinsic motivation of your student, can range from something that is merely a mild inconvenience to a big problem that interferes with your teen successfully completing the course. While there may be some value in probing why your junior does not like a particular teacher, the reality is that limiting negative personal characterizations of the teacher and keeping your student focused on the course requirements is the best strategy for overcoming this challenge. It may not be the most popular thing to say, but sometimes "suck it up, buttercup" is, in fact, the most reasonable path forward. As an adult, you can reference the fact that in any career, and in any workplace setting, we all have to learn to work effectively with people whom we may not enjoy personally or consider to be friends. Providing that mature perspective while offering personal examples can help your junior get through a class where they simply don't like the teacher.

Requesting a schedule change to avoid a disliked teacher

A question that frequently comes up when a student dislikes a teacher is, "Can't I just be assigned to a different teacher?" While this may be a viable option under certain circumstances, parents should be prepared that most of these requests are routinely declined by counselors and administrators for two valid reasons:

- Changing a student's teacher may mean undesirable changes to the student's schedule if the class must be shuffled to another period.
- Teacher sections may become unbalanced and class sizes lopsided if a student is pulled out of one class and scheduled into another.

This does not mean that switching to another teacher is never an option, but it is usually a last resort when conflicts arise. If the change request is made, the junior should take the initiative to bring that request to a counselor and have a specific rationale for doing so. In some cases, another teacher can authorize a class change *into* their section. However, in many cases, a class change once a semester has started will require an administrator override of the student's schedule.

How Do I Help My Student Resolve a Grading Dispute with a Teacher?

Make sure you and your student have read the student handbook. Most accredited high schools have detailed student handbooks with a required annual sign-off from the parent and student acknowledging receipt. The handbooks typically set forth the expected procedures and practices for student grading in detail, including how percentages translate to letter grades. Furthermore, many school districts have embedded their grading practices within their school board's adopted policies, which are usually accessible on the district website and organized topically or readily searched by keyword. These policies will address issues such as late work, partial credit, and makeup work in the event of absences due to school activities or illness.

Insist that your student take the initiative to address the grading dispute. In an effort to help students acquire the skills they will need for success as adults and to foster their ability to function independently, schools often require that juniors and seniors take the first step. This can be very challenging for a student, but it will help them acquire the resiliency and communication skills to address issues like this in the future. Encourage your student to contact the teacher before or after school and to do so in person with a request to reconsider or review an assigned grade. That request needs to have a clear rationale.

Inquire directly with the teacher only after your student has tried to resolve the issue. Send an email requesting a phone conversation at the teacher's convenience. Request an explanation of the grade, suggest the outcome you would like to see, and explain why you believe this warrants your intervention. Be prepared to listen and learn, because sometimes the teacher will reveal additional aspects related to the quality of your student's work or grading criteria that you were not aware of. Regardless of the outcome on a specific assignment, these conversations can be beneficial in helping to set the record straight and to support your student.

Because teachers are extremely busy and have limited planning time, you should allow reasonable parameters on a teacher's response time. Be patient and monitor correspondence. If you haven't heard back within 48 hours, make a follow-up phone call or send another email. If it goes another day or two and the grading dispute is still lingering with no communication from the teacher, you should escalate the request by looping in an administrator or counselor. In these cases, it may also be beneficial to request an in-person meeting with the teacher.

When Is It Appropriate to Contact an Administrator About a Conflict with a Teacher?

Sometimes a conflict with a teacher simmers too long or questions about your student's progress remain unresolved or unanswered. It may benefit your student to seek clarification by requesting that an administrator get involved in the conversation. This should never be the first line of inquiry, however, because problems are typically best resolved as close to the source as possible.

Sometimes all it takes is copying an administrator in correspondence with the teacher because it demonstrates your level of concern. In most situations, appealing to an administrator over a grading dispute is not a productive endeavor because the administrator will typically defer to the discretion of, and subject matter expertise possessed by, the teacher. However, it may provide an opportunity to convene a conversation with the assistance of an administrator who is effective at helping to resolve conflict and bring clarity where questions existed about your student's progress.

When meeting with an administrator, control what you can control. While you may be understandably frustrated about a perceived lack of responsiveness on the part of a teacher, you will not do yourself or your student any good if you are so visibly frustrated that you are lashing out with profanity or negatively characterizing the teacher or school. Think selfishly and act strategically. Recognize that maintaining your composure allows you the best opportunity to coherently state your viewpoint and to support your child.

What Can I Do to Ensure My Student Has Strong Letters of Reference and Recommendations for College Admissions and Scholarship Awards?

Here, the role of the school counselor/advisor is most important. Ideally, your junior has gotten to know their guidance counselor. Many guidance counselors take great pride in supporting students to achieve their goals for postsecondary admissions and scholarships. Counselors are typically among the most informed and expert on campus about subjects like how to successfully compile scholarship applications, how to take advantage of early admission windows for selective colleges and universities, and how to capitalize on both need- and merit-based scholarship opportunities. Take the initiative to get to know your student's counselor prior to senior year so you can start discussing post-high school plans with your junior.

Many school districts have created a common scholarship application form that can be electronically submitted. Ideally, you will have an opportunity to check out these resources online or obtain an appointment with your junior's counselor so that you can help your student be as proactive as possible in leveraging these resources.

A key element of getting the best possible letters of recommendation from teachers is for your student to equip those teachers with their résumé of activities, accomplishments, and prior awards, including reference to any volunteerism. This résumé helps teachers craft a compelling letter that can help to win scholarships, awards, and other honors. By having this information assembled in a clear and coherent fashion, your junior can start thinking about which teachers to approach as prospective references. They can update their résumé once they start their senior year.

Closing Advice

Junior year can and should be a deeply rewarding experience for your child. It hopefully reflects the positive outcome of years of persistent effort and support. Parents who are actively engaged in monitoring their student's academic progress and regularly inquiring about their social lives have a greater opportunity to help shape positive outcomes. Realistically, junior year will also create some tension as students begin to embrace their growing independence. This can often manifest as conflicts with teachers, peers, and even parents. Acknowledging that and being a present and caring force in your child's life will help your junior to not just endure, but also overcome these conflicts. With the mature perspectives and helpful assistance of caring parents who love them unconditionally, juniors will be well-equipped to take on their senior year.

Chapter 10
ONLINE PRESENCE

How to help your junior start building a career-ready profile

Timothy M. Dove
2011 and 2012 Ohio State Teacher of the Year

The beginning of 11th grade can be both exciting and frightening for an incoming junior. Students often feel like they are familiar with how to navigate high school and are often engaging in formal and informal leadership in the school. At the same time, they realize the K–12 experience is ending faster than they expected. The "what's next?" is really starting to become an ongoing consideration.

Social media and an online presence has been a part of these students' lives since they can remember. They have never known a time without personal phones, tablets, and other electronic devices with access to the internet. What a person did before electronic access is now a conversation with their grandparents. Even as I write this, I know that referencing certain devices, programs, and apps will be dated in just a few years. As an example, references to MySpace, CompuServe, Ask Jeeves, and AOL either bring a chuckle or confusion. These were the initial giants of the online landscape. This chapter will not be a history lesson, however; the point is to look at the universal issues around social media, access, and how people are perceived and use the internet to access information about each other.

Teens are digital natives and know a great deal about the electronic landscape in which they grew up, but do not confuse that with knowing everything about how it is used by others and appreciating possible unintended consequences of their online activities.

Search techniques, the use of AI, the development of basic programs/bots, and understanding the use of powerful algorithms are usually not fully appreciated by the young adult. I have even been surprised by how many do not understand or know how to protect their own personal data and location. Access as a convenience is great, but it can also be a small step toward becoming creepy. An innocuous example is when you are in a brick-and-mortar store and, as you head out for the parking lot, your phone alerts you to a possible sale in the place you just left.

Why an Online Presence Needs a Review

During my work with juniors and seniors, I taught a formal set of lessons to assist students with defining their web presence. All of us have a web presence. It has been determined through our own efforts, but also by many others, including friends, family, schools, coworkers, and even strangers. A lot of our web presence we do not even post ourselves. Whether we posted the content or someone else did, tagging us, what was "cute" or "funny" or "interesting" 10 years ago may no longer be so. Yet this information will always have a footprint on the internet. There are times in our lives when we can make a fresh start. Your student's junior year can be one of them. As they complete high school, it is time to become intentional and strategic in creating a professional adult presence on the web.

When reflecting on what a student would want as a web narrative, they need to consider the breadth of the audience. What age/generation is reviewing this web content? For what purpose would the content be reviewed? Parents can play a role in feedback and review. Often the people who are looking to fill a position for employment or offer learning opportunities are the age of parents or older, so this point of view is valuable. Other adults in the student's life with expertise, experience, or knowledge can also be helpful in this conversation.

I suggest some things to consider before your student begins this process. Remember those who review their online presence can be the very people making decisions about their future learning opportunities, employment, and professional connection years from now. Your student should be able to review and edit their online presence as time passes. A LinkedIn URL is one example that can be shared with others to showcase a student's important experiences, skills, and knowledge.

Some questions to ask your student:

- When was the last time you did a search for your name on the internet? What showed up?
- Are you happy with your current web presence (your own social media accounts and what shows up with searches of your name)?
- Do you have any ideas of how your web presence could positively or negatively affect others' perceptions of you (for employment, internships, college, military applications)?
- What else do you need to create and/or collect to present yourself online in the best way possible?

You can also share with your teen the missteps you may have made with your online presence in this process. Digital footprints do not disappear, because anyone with tech expertise can find previous posts, pictures, and information, but your student ultimately wants an avenue to push online traffic toward an updated, adult image.

Personal Control of My Own Narrative

Students can do this. People understand children make mistakes and older people will say, "I'm so glad social media was not a thing when I was growing up! I wouldn't want my life chronicled in such detail and available to anyone." Here are six step-by-step guidelines to controlling your online image:

Step 1. Select a professional name.

A good place to start to reinvent one's web presence—and this may sound weird—is for the student to decide on a professional, formal name they will be known as moving forward. Some nicknames may not be helpful in how others perceive the student.

Step 2. Use email as a way to connect.

An email account is the most basic way to communicate on the web and needs to reflect your identity as an adult rather than one that is "cute," possibly inappropriate, or from when you were eight years old. Go to an email client (such as Google) and create a new account, which should be:

- Easy to remember
- A brief address connected to your professional adult name

For example, my email address is TMDedc@gmail.com (my initials and "edc" for Education Concepts, my consulting group). Because many Gmail account names are already established, Google will make a suggestion based on what you requested and usually add a series of numbers. Don't just accept the first suggestion; play around with options that make sense. You may find something that you really like. "TDoveEd@gmail.com" will be perceived much differently than "HappyDad#1@gmail.com" or "PartyAnimal12@gmail.com." Due to its brevity, my chosen address can also be typed quickly and has less chance of being typed incorrectly. You can imagine the opportunities for error with an email address such as "ILovetoTeachmostoftheTime5321@gmail.com."

Step 3. Embrace a space to post and share.

Students should have a place to send traffic after they reset and control their personal narrative. LinkedIn is currently one such space. It is fairly simple to set up, inexpensive (free for the basic level), and gives the individual an opportunity to network with others in similar or supportive fields. According to its current usage agreement, the platform can be used by those 16 and older.

Not all social media is the same. Do not treat LinkedIn as Facebook or Instagram for the corporate world. As an example, the number of contacts you have through LinkedIn does not equate to a "the more the better" rubric. The focus is not on collecting "likes," but on making helpful contacts. Although students are quick to point out that this platform and others are "dated" or "for old people," they are used by the very people they will need and want to connect with as they move beyond high school.

Step 4. Carefully select a picture.

You would not go to a college scholarship interview or an important internship/job interview in cutoff shorts. You should present yourself in this online realm as a professional as well. Your photo could be a formal head-and-shoulders picture or you with an icon in the background, but *you* need to be the focus of the picture. There should be no group shots and *no* logos, to avoid copyright issues, assumptions, or a faux pas such as wearing an Ohio State sweatshirt while you are applying to the University of Michigan for admission or employment.

Step 5. Write a few descriptive sentences.

If you were going to introduce your professional self, what would you share? Use these as possible prompts: What holds your current interest/passion? Explain briefly why and/or what feeds this interest and/or passion? Consider your audience, and be honest. This will be a prominent part of the LinkedIn profile page.

Step 6. Set up your account.

To create a LinkedIn account, go to linkedin.com/uas/login. The website is user-friendly and walks you through the fields. A few things to keep in mind:

- Do not make up any information.
- For education, include your high school name and location and any interests (i.e., favorite classes and extracurriculars) in the "groups" section, with a short narrative.
- For employment, share any current part-time job or other experiences as an intern, coach, counselor, etc. "Student" (this is your current job and focus) needs to be included.

If the student has privacy/access issues or concerns, invite them to discuss their thoughts with you or another engaged adult, like a teacher or advisor. An example of what the final URL should look like is linkedin.com/in/tmdove. Once the account is set up, it is possible to modify on your profile page what LinkedIn gave as an initial URL to something a bit shorter and connected to the student's name.

Conversation Starters (and Answers!)

The following are conversation starters to share *after* your student has had time to think through a revamp of their web presence (with a few responses "in quotes" from my junior and senior students as they went through the process).

1. Is your LinkedIn page complete? What else might you change later and why?

    "As the school year goes on, and even beyond that as my careers as a student and employee continue, I can certainly add information as I gain it in areas such as volunteer work, organizations I have been associated with, and my employment status."

    "I may change my interests/short biography as my interests vary over time."

2. Who are your potential audiences for this page about you?

    "Job interviewers, businesses looking to hire me, or myself looking to apply to a business, colleges that I apply to, perhaps colleges that I do *not* apply to."

    "Future employers, admissions officers, and professional contacts are all potential audiences for this page."

3. What was frustrating about the experience (give any details)?

    "As a student, I felt as though I did not have as much validity in each of my accomplishments or skills, as I feel I have not developed them adequately enough to be important in the eyes of professional adults who could be viewing my page."

    "I am not good with technology; therefore, this was a little bit of a hassle."

4. When did you experience being victorious (give any details)?

"When I remembered my involvement with clubs such as drama and French, it gave me a sense of hope for my validity. I have spent so much time in these two groups that, despite their general purpose not exactly being professional in itself, my time and experience within these groups has developed into life-altering lessons that I feel are substantial enough to have an impact on my professional life."

"I experienced this when I saw other contacts I could potentially reach out to on LinkedIn."

5. Describe something you did that you believe to be effective in presenting yourself in a positive way online.

"By giving a brief synopsis of my involvement in my employment, organizations, etc., I feel that I gave another nudge to anyone viewing my page into finding me a credible person."

"I have a sophisticated and mature biography with an appropriate email to reach out to others."

6. How might this online work affect your future? Think about how this might relate to what is already there.

"As this is discovered by organizations in the future, the early growth of this page will allow it to transform and grow and, finally, mature much quicker than my peers who will not have the deep roots in this medium."

"This online work can show my progress and efforts as people message me/I message others to ask about any issues surrounding my future work."

7. What is some advice you would give to classmates/friends about this exercise?

   "I would suggest to spend perhaps an hour before beginning this page to do a self-reflection and come up with a solid list of groups they are involved in and some skills they not only gained from those positions, but also from their life."

   "I would suggest to my friends to start on this early in the year and continue to add to it and build a strong profile."

8. What did you learn about yourself in the process of creating a new online presence?

   "I realized what my passions were and how I could use them to better the world."

   "I learned that from a strictly statistical standpoint, I am quite closer to an average student than to an overachiever."

   "I learned that, there are so many different people online with different skill sets. This will help when I am trying to make connections."

   "I learned that I could do more to build my experiences and that this year will help me pursue my goals and actually create a positive influence in my community."

Closing Advice

There are some other strategies that I discovered with my own kids. In dealing with this topic, try to be more Socratic, asking questions versus telling your teen what they should do. Because they are developing independence, they do not always appreciate conversation about an area of their life over which they believe they have control.

But suggesting an adult point of view can be helpful in considering how others in the web community will view, make assumptions, and use the information. Try to connect your teen to other adults who your student values and/or perceives as having expertise in areas they'd like to pursue beyond high school.

Be careful with your own posts and comments about your student on your social media channels. You might want to consider asking permission and giving your student veto power. Continuing to demonstrate mutual respect goes a long way in building trust in your relationship.

Chapter 11
FINDING PASSIONS...IN AND OUT OF SCHOOL

How to help identify and support your teen's interests

Stacey McAdoo
2019 Arkansas State Teacher of the Year

The 11th grade is often considered a pivotal year in high school due to its significance in college preparation, academic rigor, extracurricular activities, and planning for career and college applications. As students navigate this crucial year, they face the pressures of standardized testing and the demands of advanced coursework, while also seeking to demonstrate leadership and commitment in extracurricular pursuits. However, it's never too late to explore interests and find one's passion, as the 11th grade can also be a time for self-discovery and personal growth.

Interests and passions play a critical role in the development and success of 11th graders, both in and outside the classroom. Often, pursuing one's interests and passions results in developing transferable skills that colleges and employers look for, such as self-motivation, a strong work ethic, time management, adaptability, resilience, and leadership. Putting the future benefits aside, finding one's passion also has lots of "right now" appeal. It often creates a sense of purpose and belonging and provides opportunities to help students relax and alleviate stress.

Identifying an Interest

As a parent of two very active children and an educator for 21 years, I have spent more time at school events than I have virtually anywhere else. Each time I facilitate an open house, parent night, or parent-teacher conference, I always share tips on how students can be more successful in my class and throughout their education journey in general. And, although high school is a time when most teenagers begin to crave and ask for more independence, this is an important time for parents to help their teen identify their passions and interests, both in and out of school. Here are some strategies I have shared:

1. **Encourage exploration.** Students are never too old to try new things or explore different activities. This can include signing them up for extracurricular activities, summer camps, or classes they have expressed interest in. Encourage them to try different sports, arts, or academic pursuits to see what they enjoy. These pursuits don't have to be competitive. Most schools offer a variety of clubs and intramural sports/activities that students can join. Start there.

2. **Listen to your teen.** Listen carefully to what your teen is and isn't saying. Ask open-ended questions and show genuine interest in what they have to say. This can help your teen feel heard and understood and give you insight into what they are interested in.

3. **Lead by example.** The easiest way to get a teen to identify their interests and passions is to let them see you prioritizing your interests and making time to do something you enjoy. Then, invite them to observe or participate in activities involving your interests and passions.

4. **Celebrate successes.** When a teen discovers a passion or interest, celebrate and encourage them to continue pursuing those interests. This can include attending their performances or events, displaying their artwork or creations, or simply telling them how proud you are of their accomplishments.

5. **Be patient.** Discovering passions and interests is a process that takes time, so be patient and supportive as your teen explores different activities and interests. Try not to pressure your teen to find their passion quickly; instead, focus on providing a supportive and nurturing environment for them to explore their interests.

Unlocking Your Teen's Interests and Passions

Approach conversations with your teen about their interests and passions in a supportive and respectful manner. Rather than seeking to hold them as a captive audience, it's more effective to create a conducive environment for open communication. Consider having these conversations during relaxed, one-on-one moments such as taking a walk together, over a casual meal, while riding in the car together, or engaging in an activity they enjoy. By choosing a setting where your teen feels comfortable and at ease, you can encourage an open exchange of ideas and interests. Be mindful of their schedule and emotional state, selecting a time when they are likely to be open and receptive. Providing a supportive and nonconfrontational environment can help foster a positive discussion about their interests and passions, allowing them to share their thoughts and aspirations freely. Here are some conversation starters to help your teen identify their interests and passions:

- What are some things you would do if you had unlimited time and resources?
- Is there a hobby or activity you've always wanted to try?

- What subject do you enjoy most in school?
- What do you think you're good at?
- What's something you've always wanted to learn more about?

These questions will help your junior think about their interests and passions and may spark further conversation about their goals and aspirations. It is important to let your teen lead the conversation and express their thoughts and ideas without judgment or pressure.

Managing Your Expectations

Helping your teen unlock their passions can be exciting and challenging. One of the most important things you can do during this journey is manage your expectations. Of course, we naturally want our children to share our interests and passions, but we should recognize that our teenagers probably will have different interests and desires than we do and that their interests and passions may change over time. Avoid projecting your own interests onto them. Instead, listen and support their interests. This will help your teen feel heard and understood and can also help them develop a sense of independence and self-discovery.

Encouraging experimentation with different activities and interests can help your teen discover what they enjoy and are good at. It can also help them develop a sense of curiosity and an openness to new experiences. Focus on the process, not the outcome. Appreciate the effort and hard work your teen puts into their interests. This can help your teen develop a sense of motivation and self-esteem. We often speak about celebrating diversity when trying to combat discrimination and prejudice. But when we genuinely embrace diversity, we think about it in every aspect of our lives, including our interests and passions, because everyone is unique and has their own strengths and weaknesses. By celebrating diversity, parents can create a positive and accepting environment for their child to explore their interests and passions.

"Change," as Greek philosopher Heraclitus once said, "is the only constant in life." We must be open to the idea that our child's interests and passions will change over time as they grow and develop. By being open to change and maintaining a positive attitude, we can support their growth and development in a positive and nurturing way.

Finally, seeking advice and support from other parents or professionals who can help you navigate your junior's interests and passions can be one of the most effective strategies to help manage expectations and support your teen's interests. This can include teachers, coaches, or counselors who can provide guidance and support for both you and your teen.

The Hidden Costs of Support and Commitment

When a child develops a healthy interest or passion, parents need to support and commit to helping them. This support can come in many forms, including financial, emotional, and physical.

Financial Support

1. Allocate funds. Interests and passions can be expensive. It is helpful to think of exploration and development as an investment. Therefore, allocating a portion of the household budget for equipment, classes, or lessons is wise.

2. Research scholarships. Some interests and passions may require a significant financial investment. However, grants and discounts are often available, even if they are not advertised. So, don't be afraid to ask. You may be surprised by what you discover.

3. Prioritize spending. You can prioritize spending on your child's interests over other discretionary spending. For example, you may forgo a family vacation to pay for your child's summer camp or music lessons.

Emotional Support

1. Show interest. Ask about your teen's progress, attend their performances or games, and provide encouragement and support.

2. Celebrate successes. When your teen accomplishes something related to their interest or passion, recognize their achievements. This can help build their self-esteem and reinforce their commitment to the activity.

3. Provide encouragement. Encourage and support your teen, particularly if they encounter setbacks or challenges. This can help them develop resilience and perseverance.

Physical Support

1. Provide or secure transportation. There can be a lot of driving to and from practices, lessons, and events. These activities are rarely canceled because of a long day at work or because it's raining. Having a solid transportation plan is important.

2. Create space. If possible, create a space in your home where your teen can pursue their interests and passions. It doesn't have to be an entire room, but having a designated area to spread out materials and time to practice or engage helps.

3. Participate. Include yourself in activities related to your teen's interests and passions when possible. This can include playing sports with them or attending concerts or performances together.

Commitment

1. Make time. Block off time on your calendar to ensure you can support your junior's interests and passions.

2. Be consistent. Be consistent in your support of your teen's interests and passions. This can help them develop a sense of stability and appreciate your dependability.

3. Communicate. Talk. Talk some more. Then talk again! Ask your teen about their goals (and periodically ask about their progress toward them) and aspirations related to the activity, and provide guidance and support as needed.

Closing Advice

Identifying interests, managing expectations, and supporting your teen's interests and passions requires a comprehensive approach that includes strategies for discovery, conversation starters, self-assessments, and commitment. Exploring and developing one's interests and passions can take time. But in the end, your patience, commitment, and resources are worth it when you see a return on your investment as your teen develops a sense of self-esteem, resilience, and a love of learning. Your support of and commitment to your teen's interests and passions can profoundly impact their well-being and success in life.

Self-Assessment

Checklists and self-assessments are two tools that help me tremendously in the classroom, as a parent, and in my day-to-day life. Here are some questions that can be used to help you manage your own expectations when trying to help your junior discover or identify their interests and passions:

- Am I open to my teen's interests, even if they differ from mine?
- Am I allowing my teen to explore their interests without trying to push them in a certain direction?
- Am I putting too much pressure on my teen to find their passion or achieve success in a certain area?
- Am I allowing my teen to make and learn from mistakes?
- Do I understand that my teen's interests and passions may change over time?
- Am I providing my teen a supportive environment to explore their interests and passions?
- Am I listening to my teen's thoughts and ideas without dismissing or minimizing them?
- Am I focusing on my teen's strengths and encouraging them to develop those areas?
- Am I celebrating my teen's successes, no matter how small?
- Am I remembering that my teen's journey of self-discovery is their own and not something I can control?

Chapter 12
DEVELOPING PASSIONS IN SPORTS

How to support your student-athlete

Mandy Manning
2018 National and Washington State
Teacher of the Year

I have coached basketball for several years, was a student-athlete, and have raised athletes in my home. My youngest only this year realized his passion for basketball while continuing to pursue his first love— tennis. Developing a passion for sports and being able to balance that passion with academic responsibilities is a challenge, especially for those in 11th grade. Academically, 11th grade is one of the most challenging years in high school. It is a year in which students are taking advanced classes, solidifying their college and career plans, and homing in on the activities that will launch them toward their future.

As a high school basketball coach, I expected my players to be students first and athletes second. Academic eligibility was taken very seriously, and when students fell behind, they could not play in games and often had to sit out of practice to complete assignments, finish projects, or retake exams. We also scheduled team study days, during which students caught up or moved ahead in their classes. Staying focused on academics was not a choice. It was a requirement.

Developing a passion for sports in 11th grade requires a realistic perspective. By 11th grade, those athletes with the skills and ability to play beyond high school are usually making the varsity team for their sport. Sometimes, athletes playing junior varsity in 11th grade simply need additional training and skill development to move to the next level. Those with a true passion for their sport are usually willing to put in the extra time and effort to develop their athletic talent and maintain academic progress. To support your child in pursuing their passion, staying healthy, and maintaining balance, you need to provide honesty (probably the most difficult part), guidance with scheduling and good health habits, and financial support.

Developing and Maintaining Passion

Developing and maintaining a passion for sports requires mental toughness and tenacity. A student-athlete must maintain their confidence while building skill. A passion for sports does not always come from intrinsic talent. For some athletes, pursuing their passion means an extra focus on skill development and training. Every athlete must have **a growth mindset**, because engaging in competitive sports requires practice, and even the best athlete on the team still has skills to learn.

Additionally, failure is common in sports, whether it comes in the form of losing games or not performing to the best of one's ability. **Failure needs to be a learning opportunity**; otherwise, failure can extinguish passion in seconds. Student-athletes need support in confronting and overcoming challenges and staying focused even when they fail. It can be difficult for athletes to stay focused when they plateau in their performance or when they are on a losing streak. Tell your child that failure is an opportunity to improve and, without failure, victory would not feel as satisfying. Failure helps us identify where we need to focus our practice and effort. Find a story or two online about an athlete who overcame early adversity to find success in their sport.

Goal setting is a critical part of maintaining passion for a sport. Student-athletes must decide what they hope to accomplish through their sport and the steps necessary to get there. Setting short-term and long-term goals is important. The long-term goal depends on how far they desire to go with their sport. The goal might be to play on the varsity team, play at the collegiate level, or maybe they hope to coach the sport one day. Short-term goals should serve their long-term goal, encompassing the necessary steps to get there. For example:

- To make the varsity team, develop skills for a specific position and/or have a goal for reaching a certain number of points or rebounds/tackles in a game.
- To work toward the collegiate goal, aim to make the varsity team by junior year.
- To work toward coaching, offer to coach at a youth summer camp.

As student-athletes move through their short-term goals, they should reflect on the process and how they better meet their next goal based on what they learned. Along with goals for their sport, student-athletes also need academic goals to help them stay focused on their classes, maintain their grades, and prioritize their schoolwork. Success in sports can be a powerful motivator for doing well academically. Support your student-athlete in the goal-setting process through encouragement and an organizational structure that you help them with.

> ### Collegiate Sports
>
> If playing at the college level is your child's goal, it is essential to understand how college recruitment and access works. Help your child find out how to take their game to the next level and possibly earn scholarships. They will need to know which programs they are interested in pursuing and how to do so, which means you both need to learn about eligibility requirements and recruitment practices and policies for their school(s) of choice. Learn more about these requirements from the National Collegiate Athletic Association (NCAA), which governs this area, at ncaa.org. Encourage your student-athlete to visit campuses, because 11th grade is a critical year for exploring college options and waiting until senior year may be too late. Your child will also need to develop highlight videos of skills and competition that they can provide to recruiters. Learn more about these reels at ncsasports.org/college-recruiting-video.

Finally, passion also requires love. Playing a sport should be enjoyable. If a sport no longer brings joy, it is time to reassess and determine if that passion should be retired or can be reignited. Student-athletes need the most support when they are faced with waning passion. Support your child in asking honest questions, reflecting, and making the hard choice between sticking with a sport they no longer enjoy but have put so much time and energy into or leaving it behind to pursue other passions. You could ask:

- Do you still enjoy playing this sport?

- Do you still have the same desire to play?
- Are you excited for practice?
- Do you look forward to games or look for other opportunities to play?
- Do you still see yourself playing this sport next year? Why or why not?
- Will it serve you to stick with it? Will it serve the team?
- What are the pros and cons of sticking with this sport?

Considerations for Pursuing a Passion for Sports

Student-athletes should focus on continued skill development and conditioning throughout the year and during the summer. They should engage in regular practice and training. They should stay physically fit, build strength, endurance, agility, and flexibility. They need to be well-rounded to excel in their chosen sport. Continuous training that includes stretching, good nutrition and hydration, and time for recovery will help them improve as an athlete, as well as prevent injuries. Taking care of their body will ensure they have longevity in their sport.

Pursuing passion in sports requires practice beyond the high school season. Many student-athletes play multiple sports throughout the school year. However, by 11th grade, it should be clear to your teen and you which sport they are most passionate about and whether they hope to pursue it beyond high school. If they do, it is critical to begin focusing solely on that sport year-round if your teen has not done so already. This focus requires participating in leagues outside of school and seeking additional practice, coaching, and mentoring in the offseason and competing in matches, tournaments, and games whenever possible, including attending camps during the summer.

Keep in mind that leagues and camps can be quite costly in terms of money and time.

How to Support Your Student-Athlete

Being a student-athlete requires focus, commitment, and balance. Being passionate about a sport means spending a significant amount of time practicing and prioritizing that sport. Student-athletes have to make sacrifices in their social lives, commit to healthy living, and make positive choices that serve them athletically and academically. Here is a list of five basic supports to help your teen stay on track:

1. **Establish routines.** Teach your junior how to manage their sport and school schedules, and still have time for a social life. Student-athletes need to understand fully what it takes to be a committed athlete and how to ensure that they are mentally and physically ready for the demands they will face. Balance is critical and time management is critical to balance.

2. **Communicate with teachers and coaches.** One way student-athletes fall behind is by not checking progress regularly through communicating with their teachers and coaches. Help your junior create a system for checking in with those helping them pursue their passion. However, do not take over. Allow your teen to be their own advocate. Be supportive and understanding while promoting independence.

3. **Provide resources.** In addition to goal setting, provide the resources your teen needs to effectively pursue their passion. These resources can come in the form of financial support for leagues and camps; help accessing additional skills development through coaching, videos, or books; and/or providing equipment and time to practice.

4. **Monitor stress levels.** Provide quiet space and time to rest and complete schoolwork. Promote healthy living. Ensure your teen has nutritious meals and snacks that are also quick so they can eat well on the go. Encourage rest and recovery.

5. **Celebrate achievements.** Attend your teen's sporting events and celebrate their victories both in the classroom and on the field or court.

Closing Advice

Above all, student-athletes need to demonstrate good sportsmanship and teamwork. They should work to develop their skills to be a good teammate and support other players in doing the same. Help your teen develop compassion and empathy and teach them how to build up their teammates. Playing a team sport can be frustrating if every player is not doing their best. Remind your teen that they only have control over their own training and performance and should only work to build passion in their teammates, not tear them down. Help your teen recognize that if they are going out there and giving their all for the team and themselves, then they have won.

Conversation Starters

- What do you love most about [insert sport]? What about it brings you joy and fulfills you?

- Thinking about this sport, what are two or three goals you would like to achieve this year? How can I support you in achieving those goals?

- How will you balance your sport, schoolwork, family, and social obligations? What can we do here at home to help you manage your time?

- Do you want to play this sport in college? What will you need to do to improve your skills to move to the next level? What kind of commitment are you willing to make and what will that look like?

- Along with attending practice, what else do you need to do to grow as an athlete and stay healthy in mind and body? How can we help facilitate nutrition and conditioning at home?

- How can we support you as you face the challenges of your sport (which include potential injuries and impact to academic performance) and make hard decisions if/when the time arises?

Chapter 13

IS YOUR STUDENT A BUDDING ARTIST?

How to help your teen pursue a life in the arts

Lisa Hirkaler
NBCT Art Educator, 2016 New Jersey County Teacher of the Year

There are so many expectations during 11th grade. For arts-focused students hoping to study at the university level, there is the expectation of building an academic and creative life. Art created at the highest academic level, with the ultimate acknowledgement of excellence through academic art scholarship, is difficult and highly competitive. In this chapter, I'll lay out several concrete ways arts-focused 11th graders can begin to establish their creative identity both in and out of school, with an eye to pursuing art in the future. As a painter, sculptor, and veteran visual arts teacher, I will focus on the visual arts, but rest assured that I have all the arts in mind, including music, theater, and performing arts.

The Portfolio

Arts-focused students may be perfectly comfortable with the high-stakes testing of junior year, but some are not. It is important to remember that tests are only one part of a well-rounded application, and there are ways to establish your qualifications to higher-level study without them. I have art-inclined sons: One studied with professional SAT and math coaches and the other said "no" to standardized testing. Art-inclined students should be aware that dedicated art schools may waive the SAT requirement. Larger universities with outstanding art programs may still require SAT/ACT scores, which will be in combination with a portfolio or performance review that represents your creative growth. Arts-focused students should be shaping their college application lists with this difference in mind. Some will feel strongly about art schools, while others will seek the full university experience, which combines traditional academics with their artistic focus. Dedicated art schools are very competitive, so preparing a portfolio early is key to admission. These institutions are willing to provide campus visits, portfolio reviews, advice on admissions, and advice on courses to take before final decisions are made.

Shows, Competitions, and Recitals

An important way to begin to establish your portfolio is offered in the art shows, concerts, theatrical shows, and performances that happen during the fall, holiday season, and spring. A student can show work in class, school, high school shows—especially National Art Honor Society shows—country- and statewide shows, and at their board of education, town or city hall, or local library. In New Jersey, for example, William Paterson University hosts art shows for high school juniors and seniors. This show has provided full and partial scholarships, college acceptances, and portfolio reviews. At the NJ Education Association, our teacher's union, students can show their work, too.

Usually, 10 to 12 works of art are required for a strong portfolio. However, five to six excellent works can be presented, along with works in progress, thoughtful sketchbooks, photography, and/or photographs of sculptures.

Students who are interested in arts-based schools should actively seek out these show experiences, as they indicate a level of achievement and often provide incentives in the form of arts academic scholarships. During the last 25-plus years of teaching visual art, I have encouraged students to try to exhibit their work in these highly competitive shows. Students not only can win prizes—ranging from free summer workshops to full-tuition scholarships—but they also get a strong résumé item showing commitment to the arts. Art schools are eager to recruit talented high school students at regional shows, and I have had 10 students receive extensive scholarships, ranging from a few hundred dollars to an offering of more than $20,000 per year for four years. Juniors should reach out to their teachers to find out about deadlines and dates for shows.

Recommendation Letters

Recommendation letters are a key part of any college application, but you have to keep in mind the intended audience, which is a university admissions committee seeking to understand what this student will add to the school's program. Students should reach out to at least three teachers and guidance counselors to ask for letters of recommendation in the early fall. Many students wait until late in the application process, and then it is more difficult for teachers to give the time needed for a thoughtful letter. Most of the digital application platforms require three letters. At my school, these letters are sent digitally by the school and kept on file with the guidance office. I would suggest asking for one hard copy sealed in an envelope, just in case you need to send in a hard copy application via snail mail.

Your student should make the process easy for the people writing the recommendations by offering a sheet that lays out expectations in applying to college, overall GPA, arts GPA, accomplishments and awards, and things that are important to the student outside of class. This information helps teachers write a balanced recommendation with detail that brings out the special qualities of each student and allows admissions committees to see how the student will fit into their program.

Art Classes and Clubs

I am often asked, "How can a parent support a child's artistic interests, while also helping them achieve academically?" The answer is that these two paths are not opposed. **To the arts-minded student, art courses and after-school clubs are key to their core education.** Art students take these courses in school to grow. They see their art discipline as their "voice," and the art rooms as places to express themselves and thrive. Traditionally, academic students also benefit from a creative experience for these same reasons and should be welcome in the art room. Visual arts classes are usually safe, nurturing spaces. Most students are in art classes to experience, express, and seek hands-on work in media different from their written academic classes.

Beyond the school classroom, art classes and after-school clubs create a space where students "find their people," their vibe, their artsy tribe…in other words, their community of like minds: the creatives and a teacher who understands them. Getting involved in after-school clubs or activities and staying involved through junior and senior years is a key résumé item to add to college applications. This goes for the other arts as well. Musical performance and theatre art classes are geared toward a community of disciplined students working together to reach show goals. Theatre students often feel as though they've found their school family.

Visiting Galleries and Museums

One of my favorite things to do with my students is to visit museums and galleries. I try to gather information before visiting. I read and research so I know a bit of the background about the works. I prepare lessons for my art and AP art history students to guide their exploration of the art on view. Most students enjoy creating a slideshow featuring some of their favorite works, and they include a brief explanation about what interests them about each one. I love to visit new museums when I travel, too. My advice is to visit the gift shop first. There you will find postcards that usually represent the most popular works featured at that museum. I like to purchase the cards and take notes on the backs.

Visit art museums, galleries, and art fairs. Encourage your art student to spend time in front of their favorite pieces and take mental or physical notes on the works that appeal to them. Explore artists that are similar in style. Your student can follow up with further reading and videos. You can offer supplies so your student can experiment with a similar material or style.

I am in a rural location with very few cultural centers, yet I am lucky enough to be a little more than an hour from New York City and all its museums, including the Metropolitan Museum of Art (the Met) and the Museum of Modern Art (MoMA). I am also a professional artist affiliated with the Pleiades Gallery in the Chelsea Arts District in New York City. Visiting contemporary galleries will offer a full range of art that is thought-provoking, made with all sorts of materials, and often sublime.

Finished Pieces

The admissions committees who review portfolios are interested in finished work, so it is important for parents and teachers to provide the time and space for students to produce mature work. As early as sophomore year, teens can be asked to think about their medium. Are they interested in two dimensions or three? Painting, photography, sculpture, or digital art?

Offer to set up space to try different media. For example, perhaps your teen can set up a painting area at home. Most teachers are willing to send clay home with students and then fire the works at school. Your student should ask their teacher for advice on working at home with oils and watercolor vs. pastels, graphite, and charcoal; on manipulating an armature, clay, and glaze; on what tools to use; and on rules for keeping the work damp so they can transport the work back to school. Of course, this is something that could be done in class or after school, but it is rewarding to see the work come to fruition at home, where you can encourage your child with words of affirmation.

Art schools and colleges really understand the time, effort, and patience required to produce finished work. Artists know how much time and practice goes into excellent craftsmanship, and we gain a deeper respect for those masters of the arts found in museums and galleries. An 11th-grade art student must concentrate on finishing work and getting ready for a fully developed portfolio. The arts portfolio must have a focus and be ready to present to college administrators. In my son's portfolio review, he included several pencil renderings, a few watercolor paintings, one abstract painting, a self-portrait, photographs of nature, his full sketch pad, and photographs of his wheel-thrown pottery. Other students might include six fully developed paintings and works in progress with notes to discuss their ideas. This leaves room for the college representative to offer guidelines, ideas, and suggestions for acceptance into their program. A junior has time to develop a strong body of finished work.

Closing Advice

A successful arts application involves the usual junior year tests, recommendations, and proof of personal growth, but also, crucially, the student's portfolio. You can help your teen envision their possible future, and lower their stress, by guiding them to think about these things in 11th grade. Enjoy the process and enjoy providing them with too many supplies, lessons, and experiences.

Conversation Starters

- When choosing your classes for junior and senior years, how have you considered the balance between arts-focused classes and AP/honors classes?

- Can you schedule time with your studio art teacher to review your portfolio?

- Do you see yourself going to an arts-focused college or a more traditional academic college?

- Which university towns or cities would you like to visit, and are there museums or galleries there you'd like to visit?

- Which teachers are on your list to reach out to for college recommendations and why?

- Which teachers would you like to ask to help with your college essay?

Chapter 14
READY FOR 12TH GRADE?

How to support your soon-to-be high school senior

Lori Knisley
2015 Ohio State Teacher of the Year

The end of junior year brings both elation and anxiety, as students look forward to their senior year of high school. While your student is likely eager to return in the fall, having *finally* reached the top of the pecking order and looking forward to events such as prom and graduation, there may be some underlying trepidation. With established school routines in place, a network of friends, and the support of families at home, the very idea of leaving the comfort and safety of school to participate in the adult world can be daunting. Because more students are suffering from anxiety than ever before, taking proactive steps to support your child's overall well-being by celebrating the highs and mitigating the lows of preparing for senior year will be critical.

We want our children to be healthy, happy, and successful, yet as they get older, we may feel a bit distant from or shut out of their day-to-day lives (especially their school lives) as they seek more autonomy. This makes it harder to sense or identify signs of unhappiness or struggle. As young adults, they want to make their own choices and lead independent lives, but that can be scary for both them and us. Admittedly, while relinquishing any degree of power in our parent-child dynamic doesn't come easy, it is necessary to foster independence, critical thinking, and our kids' ability to be resilient, confident, and prepared for next year and beyond. Essentially, this is a critical time for **connection**, **reflection**, and **ongoing support**.

Connection

My children all attended the public school where I have taught English for the last 22 years, so I had an advantage over many parents. Not only did I drive them each day, which provided me with the chance to engage in quick conversations about their classes, to follow up to make sure they had completed and remembered their homework, to ask how their friends were doing, and to discuss any upcoming plans, but more importantly, I had immediate and direct access to each of their teachers, as well as their guidance counselor and extracurricular advisors. While this wasn't a thrill for my oldest son, who pretended he didn't know me (even when he was in my AP English literature classroom), my daughter and my youngest son didn't seem to mind the intrusion into their school lives, which included working with some of their friends, either as students in my class or as coaches in our writing center. Through it all, I got a very honest and accurate picture of how others perceived my children: the good, the bad, and the ugly.

Ultimately, what I discovered was the power of connections. More than just maintaining open communication with my children, connecting with their interests, friends, teachers, coaches, club advisors, and counselors helped provide a holistic snapshot of their academic and personal progress. Fortunately, you don't need to become a teacher to achieve the same thing. School personnel today have greater access to technology than ever before, so it's easy to connect. Your child's

Connection Checklist for 11th Grade

Early Fall
- ☐ Attend open house/meet the teacher night.
- ☐ Review teen's schedule and discuss any concerns.
- ☐ Subscribe to school and/or classroom apps for important information.
- ☐ Complete and return forms sent from school.

Ongoing
- ☐ Connect with extracurricular advisors and/or coaches.
- ☐ Attend school activities and/or events important to teen.
- ☐ Connect with classroom teachers.
- ☐ Connect with guidance counselor.
- ☐ Attend parent-teacher conferences.
- ☐ Review grades periodically; don't wait for report cards to post.
- ☐ Discuss teen's interests and plans for the future.

Spring
- ☐ Review ACT and/or SAT scores to determine if retesting may be beneficial.
- ☐ Schedule college visits, if applicable.
- ☐ Help teen apply for early admission consideration at universities.
- ☐ If teen plans to enlist, schedule ASVAB with recruiter (see page 120).
- ☐ If teen is in a career and technical education (CTE) course, ensure they are on track to earn credentials, credits, or graduation seals.

teacher may write a blog, provide access to a classroom website, or use some other educational technology to communicate with students and families. With many school districts using apps such as Remind or ClassDojo or platforms such as Google Classroom, connecting through messaging and/or email is both efficient and valuable.

Never hesitate to reach out to your child's teachers to develop a partnership, as the most successful students are those whose parents and teachers collaborate to support learning and personal growth. If you have a talent or skill that may be beneficial in a particular class or discipline, share that information with your student's teachers. Educators love inviting community members into classrooms to engage with students and are always receptive to hearing from parents, so be sure to reach out with any questions, concerns, or even suggestions you may have to help your student engage in the work necessary to successfully complete courses and feel confident and prepared for senior year.

Reflection

My children are now adults in their mid- to late-20s, yet I still vividly recall each of them in the final months of their junior year of high school. While each held different expectations and hopes for senior year, my oldest son and daughter were similar in wanting to ensure they had scheduled all the necessary classes for graduation, while padding their schedule with fun electives; they were deliberate in their choices and confident that their senior year would be great. Both had determined that they would pursue a college degree, so we began talking about potential majors, visiting universities for tours, the viability of out-of-state attendance, the cost of enrollment, and the importance of finishing senior year strong. My youngest son, on the other hand, wasn't looking that far into the future. He was struggling with the decision to stay in a career and technical education (CTE) program that he had begun at the start of junior year. His concern was that his English class didn't have the rigor and high expectations of the honors courses he had taken as a freshman and sophomore. As his junior year progressed, he expressed concern about his learning, saying he felt he might be unprepared to enroll in a four-year liberal arts school after graduation.

As a parent and teacher, I had mixed emotions about the situation. I didn't want to dissuade him from completing the program, as he seemed to enjoy the classes and was working with his hands and gaining practical work experience. But as a teacher, I knew he would need a solid foundation in reading, writing, and public speaking if he wanted to be successful in his first year of college if that were the path he chose to follow.

In order to reach a resolution, my son and I sat down and discussed his concerns. As a parent, it's natural to want to offer answers and immediate solutions, but if we do so only from our perspective, we eliminate our child's ability to exercise sound judgment and good decision-making as it relates to making personal choices. While I desired to ease his mind and bolster his confidence, I realized he needed to arrive at his own conclusions because critical thinking, self-reflection, and good decision-making are fundamental to personal growth and academic success.

Because most teenagers are not fully confident in making decisions on their own, guiding your child toward self-reflective practices could be useful. You can use four steps:

1. **Model positive thinking and decision-making.** Share with your teen a time when you found something to be a struggle or you failed at something. Honestly describe how you overcame the situation. Did you call on someone for assistance

or exercise autonomy in rectifying the situation? How did the experience strengthen your resolve and lead to greater understanding of your own abilities, skills, and talents? Help your teen begin an inner dialogue with questions like:

- "I wonder what would happen if I?" to allow them to envision the future.
- "How did I feel when…?" to validate feelings and motivations.
- "What might have happened if I had?" to aid in learning from mistakes through critical thinking and reflection.

2. **Reinforce a growth mindset.** As a student, I dreaded trigonometry; tangents and cosines seemed like a foreign language, and math just seemed hard. Thankfully, I met a teacher who changed my thinking. He taught me that challenges can be overcome and that I simply needed to believe that I could succeed in order to begin dismantling the barriers that had been preventing my growth. Help your teen reflect on past learning to identify personal areas of struggle and set academic and/or personal goals for growth. While these goals can be shared with teachers, counselors, or coaches, the most important thing is that your teen assumes responsibility for their learning and engages in monitoring progress toward reaching desired goals. Then, help them maintain their motivation.

3. **Mitigate the lows.** When setbacks occur, remind your teen of their goals, the progress made to that point, and urge patience. Today's culture supports instant gratification—information is available at our fingertips, movies and television shows are on demand—but true personal growth takes time. Help your teen identify something positive from the experience that can become a useful tool for future success. Remind your teen that perseverance and resilience are the reward of pushing through challenges and they help to develop a growth mindset.

4. **Celebrate accomplishments.** Take time to acknowledge your student's successes, both big and small. Whether it is completing an assignment on time, overcoming a fear of public speaking to present to the class, scoring well on an assessment, or just making it to school every day, let your student know that you are proud of their efforts.

Promoting self-reflection requires open and honest communication and strengthens resilience and builds autonomy, which will be critical for senior year. Ultimately, my son was able to weigh the pros and cons of his career program and determined that a compromise could be reached if he were permitted to take AP English in his senior year rather than the English course embedded in his CTE program. He felt confident in his choice, but more than a little anxious to find out if this would be possible. With some encouragement, he spoke to his guidance counselor the next day. In the end, he was relieved to find out that he could drop an elective and pick up AP English, fully meeting all requirements for graduation; as a parent, I was thrilled that he took ownership of his learning and advocated for himself.

Ongoing Support

Use the connections made with school personnel through attendance at open house, meet the teacher night, parent-teacher conferences, or school events to support your teen's ongoing personal development and academic growth.

There are some additional steps that can be taken to ensure that your student is ready for senior year. First, review graduation requirements and help your teen make informed choices for senior year. Each year, guidance counselors are required to meet with students to discuss college, career training, or enlistment after graduation.

Talk with your teen about their plans after high school, and help keep them on track. With new graduation pathways developed in recent years, it's vital to know which avenue your teen must take to meet their postsecondary goals.

Plans for college: If you are considering different majors, help your child make important decisions related to course selections for senior year. Many schools offer Advanced Placement (AP), College Credit Plus (CCP), International Baccalaureate (IB), and honors classes. So what's the difference and how can this help?

1. AP classes provide college-level curricula and typically require or strongly recommend participants sit for the AP exam in May; the exams may be offered free or at a reduced rate, if eligible, or require payment of $98 per exam. A student must typically score a 3, 4, or 5 on an AP exam to earn three college credits in the subject area; select schools may require a score of 4 or 5. With the average cost per credit hour at $293 for in-state residents at state universities, college credit earned through AP can provide a huge savings.

   Yet, according to College Board Research, in "New Analyses Find Students Who Earn a 2 on an AP Exam Are Prepared for the Rigor of College Courses," published July 23, 2021, "New evidence shows that AP students who earn scores of 2 on their AP exams have significantly stronger college outcomes than similar students who did not take an AP course and exam." The figures in that news release show that "AP students, including those with average scores of 1 or 2, are more likely to enroll in a four-year college" and "are well-prepared to succeed in introductory college coursework, frequently outperforming academically similar college peers who did not take the AP course in high school."

2. CCP courses may either be taken on the high school campus with a teacher who is registered as an adjunct with a local college

or on a university campus. These courses are generally required first-year college courses. Districts provide the financing so that students who successfully pass the class do not have to pay tuition, and because the students are dual-enrolled, they earn high school graduation and college credits. This can save both time and money in completing a university degree. However, a student who earns less than a C may be ineligible for college credit and/or may have to pay college tuition for the course.

3. The IB Diploma Programme is an internationally recognized curriculum that offers 11th and 12th graders the opportunity to earn an IB diploma or individual IB certificates. To earn the diploma, students must complete assessments in six IB subjects, write an extended essay of independent study, complete creativity, activity, and service experiences, and participate in a critical thinking course. Students who take individual courses can earn certificates by testing, and these certificates generally reflect a student's area of interest and academic strength. Not all colleges recognize IB courses, but the higher level (HL) courses usually show more rigor than the standard level (SL).

4. Honors classes require students to work within a curriculum that is at an advanced level of high school. These courses often have prerequisites that must be met to ensure students have the right foundation for learning. If, for example, your child is considering a career in the medical field, a class such as Honors Anatomy could give your child an advantage when entering college as a freshman.

The advantages of taking AP, CCP, IB, or honors coursework may include weighted grades and an indication of college readiness to admissions officers. The overall grade point average (GPA) of students who successfully complete these courses may exceed the standard 4.0 scale, which may help with admission to select schools and/or generate scholarship opportunities. A final high school transcript that includes a number of rigorous courses indicates to university admissions officers that the proposed candidate is committed to learning and will probably be successful.

Students who are college-bound should also consider:

- Job shadowing opportunities in junior and/or senior year of high school
- College visits in junior and/or senior year of high school
- Preparation for auditions and/or walk-on tryouts at universities of interest
- Exploration of work-study programs at universities of interest
- Discussion about living in a dorm versus an apartment

Plans for career: If your child prefers to enter the work world after graduation, you can assist with the transition. Encourage your student to meet with teachers and/or the guidance counselor to explore opportunities such as:

- Job shadowing in junior or senior year
- Apprenticeships or journeyman programs after completing a CTE course
- Micro-credentialing, or graduation seals, earned through a CTE program

Plans for enlistment: If your child wants to enlist in the armed forces, have them talk with their guidance counselor or a recruiter about taking the Armed Services Vocational Aptitude Battery (ASVAB). This test is typically available to students in the fall of each school year through the Department of Defense's Career Exploration Program, which is designed to help students explore both civilian and military careers.

The more information your teen gathers, the greater their confidence will be as they prepare for senior year.

Closing Advice

Just as families explore their roots through ancestry, students can trace connections made over time and through various disciplines during the course of their educational journey, a journey that began when a seed was planted and nurtured: the notion that your child would grow into a formidable young adult. Rooted in the love and support of family, this seed soon sprouted and reached toward the sun, where parents and guardians continue to foster the inquisitive and creative mind while shaping beliefs, ideals, morals, and perspectives. Through continued nurturing of the seedling, your child entered the world a tender green shoot, fragile and innocent. Educators were entrusted with the care and maintenance of the emerging sapling, hoping to inspire creativity, critical thinking, and learning through hands-on play and social interaction with same-age peers. With parents and educators working in partnership, the sapling, growing more resilient and reaching higher toward the sky, became more deeply rooted in the rich and fertile soil that nourished it. As your child continues to grow, like a tree reaching its many limbs outward and upward to claim its rightful place in the sky, they may be pushing boundaries and seeking independence. Yet the roots, which have always remained out of sight, continue to grow along with the tree. So, as you find yourself confronted with a young and mighty oak, take a moment to reflect on the beauty that is your child. The root system is strong and there is a long life ahead.

www.ingramcontent.com/pod-product-compliance
Lightning Source LLC
Chambersburg PA
CBHW011758040426
42446CB00018B/3456